THE
GREAT
PEACEMAKER

This photograph shows General Robert in his study at the age of 86.

THE
GREAT
PEACEMAKER

By
RALPH C. SMEDLEY L.H.D.

TOASTMASTERS INTERNATIONAL
Santa Ana, California

Los Angeles
BORDEN PUBLISHING COMPANY
1955

PRINTED IN THE UNITED STATES OF AMERICA

LIBRARY OF CONGRESS CATALOGUE CARD NUMBER 55-11372

Acknowledgments

Sincere appreciation is due to Mrs. Sarah Corbin Robert for her aid in making available helpful information concerning General Robert's life and work.

Quotations from *Robert's Rules of Order, Revised,* are used with the permission of Mrs. Robert, Trustee and of Scott, Foresman and Company, Publishers.

Quotations from *Parliamentary Law* are included by permission of Appleton-Century-Crofts, Inc.

Contents

I. WHY A PEACEMAKER?   9
    Family Background

II. CONSTRUCTING THE CAREER   17
    West Point — The Northwest

III. FIRST VENTURE IN CHAIRMANSHIP   22
    The Officer Becomes a Student — Out West Again

IV. THE BEGINNING OF THE RULES   26
    Laying the Foundation — Erecting the Structure

V. PUBLICATION AT LAST   35
    *Plan of the Book — Parliamentarian Becomes
    Publisher — The Authority*

VI. FURTHER STUDIES OF ORDERLY
PROCEDURE   50
    A Family of Parliamentarians — Later Publications

VII. ROBERT REBUILDS A CITY   59
    *Creation of the Harbor at Galveston — The Storm —
    The Seawall*

VIII. YEARS OF RETIREMENT   67
    Robert the Man

IX. APPENDIX   76
    *The Rules Are Simple
    The President
    The Secretary
    Standardization*

CHAPTER I

Why A Peacemaker?

It may appear that this is a strange title to be conferred on a man who spent his active life in military service, wearing the uniform of the United States Army and serving as an Army Engineer. It is well deserved, however, for Henry Martyn Robert was the author of a book which has prevented or stopped a million fights.

It is impossible even to guess how many disputes have been dissolved, how many arguments have been settled, how much time has been saved, how much transaction of business has been made possible by reference to that familiar little book, *Robert's Rules of Order*. The general acceptance of the *Rules* as the authority in matters of procedure in meetings has expedited the work of assemblies of all kinds, and all organizations profit from it.

General Robert was and is a great promoter of peaceful procedure, whenever people get together to work cooperatively.

But who was Robert, and by what authority do his *Rules* govern us? No legislative assembly has ever enacted his laws and made them a legal prescription, except as it has adopted them for its own guidance. Yet we follow his regulations unquestioningly, and yield to his opinion on every point in our group affairs.

Although he died years ago, he still hands down decisions, rules our assemblies, and writes a paragraph into the constitution or bylaws of almost every organization, and his book is a perennial staple on the shelves of the book sellers. Why is this so? What is the reason for his influence and authority?

Such questions as these led me to look into the life of the man behind the *Rules*, to see who he was, and by what authority he wrote. For most of my life I had been one of his followers, without ever knowing why, except that it was the custom. Certainly I had a right to know something about him.

But when I started my search for information, to my amazement I found that very little was available in any collected form. It seemed incredible that a man whose work has been so influential in human affairs could have been so completely overlooked. Because there was so little to be found, I extended my efforts and was led into far-reaching studies and research, the results of which appear in this book.

What I have managed to assemble in the way of a story of the life and character of this great man is inadequate, but it has given me some understanding of the work of General Robert and of the reasons why his system of procedure has been so generally accepted. The material presented in these pages has been gathered from many sources which I count reasonably authentic. It appears to be the most comprehensive collection of information on the subject which has as yet been made available to the public.

It has been my purpose to humanize the *Rules* and their author and to find answers to some of the questions in my own mind. It is probable that other followers of the *Rules* have asked similar questions. In that case, here are some of the answers.

My experience as a member of an organization began in the 1890's when I joined a young people's society in the church which I attended. This brought about my introduction to formal procedure in conducting meetings. I learned that people did not speak out of turn, and that business was transacted by means of motions and votes.

Some impulse led me to wonder about the workings of the club which had received me as a member. I borrowed the secretary's book and read the constitution and bylaws. In the bylaws I found a paragraph which provided that in case any matter arose which was not covered by the rules of the society, *Robert's Rules of Order* should be accepted as final authority.

Reading the provision without great care, I made the mistake which millions of other people have made in thinking of the writer's name as Roberts instead of Robert. It was not until I began this study that I finally came to realize the difference.

That youthful experience brought me for the first time in contact with Robert and his *Rules*. I did not know who he was, nor did I feel any curiosity on that point. He was named as an authority, and I accepted him as such. My associates did the same.

We took his *Rules of Order* as something foreordained and inevitable, like the weather, or the measles, or the Constitution of the United States. Our bylaws said he was the "authority" and that settled it.

The only copy of the *Rules* in our Illinois village was owned by the principal of the school. He carried the book to meetings in his pocket, and was our main dependence when questions of conduct arose. No doubt his copy was one of the earliest editions, for the *Rules* had been in circulation only a short time. The book was published in 1876, so within sixteen years after its initial appearance it had won recognition as the final authority. A provision to that effect was found in the bylaws of most organizations even at that early date, just as it was in the bylaws of our society.

The earliest edition in my possession today was printed in 1880. It is one of the thirtieth thousand published. I never cease to marvel at the way it gained attention and circulation in a day when the publishing and distribution of books was so much more leisurely than it has become in more recent times. A book which sold thirty thousand copies in four years, back in those early times, must have established a notable record in the publishing field.

That record has been maintained through the years, and the book which started in so spectacular a fashion still holds its place as a steady seller in all the bookstores.

The price of the book kept me from becoming the owner of a copy in those early years. I had to content myself with information gained at second hand or from a borrowed copy.

But all through the years I have yielded Robert and his *Rules* my loyal and unquestioning obedience. As a member of various organizations, and as chairman from time to time, my conduct has been subject to his dictates.

My active interest in the work of the Toastmasters Clubs led to careful study of the *Rules*, for experience in chairmanship was one of the principles on which the clubs operated. We accepted *Robert's Rules* in all points, and followed him faithfully and with gratitude. Training in parliamentary procedure has always been one of our objectives, and Robert has been our guide.

There came a day when I grew bold enough to inquire about the source of this authority. I asked, "Who is Robert that I should follow him, and whence came the right of these rules to command me?"

With confidence I went to the encyclopedia, and then to the reference library, never doubting that the life of one who rules the official activities of millions of people would have been interpreted by many writers. To my amazement, I found almost nothing. Aside from the fact that General Henry Martyn Robert was the author of Robert's *Rules of Order* and that he died in 1923, my search was fruitless.

Thus, it appeared that the man who had written one of America's best sellers, who had prescribed methods of procedure for countless organizations, and whose opinions were absolute law to millions, had been completely overlooked by biographers. Certainly he is entitled to better treatment. I went to work to discover the facts.

My quest for information led me to dusty army records, to chance references and allusions in magazines and newspapers, to former acquaintances of his, and finally to members of his family, who were helpful in making available some of the material here presented.

As an example of my method of research, let me say that one of the first real leads was found in *Who's Who* for 1923, which carried a paragraph about General Robert, noting his death. This paragraph mentioned the fact that his residence in recent years had been in Owego, New York. That gave me a starting point.

I wrote to the Secretary of the Rotary Club in Owego, inquiring whether any members of the family still resided in that city. This brought a response which put me in touch with Mrs. Isabel H. Robert, the General's widow, who gave me much helpful information and started me on more extensive investigations. It required careful study of incidents and opinions to determine which were authentic and illuminating, as I conferred by mail with various sources of information.

Every effort has been made to ascertain the reliability of the facts here presented. While there may be minor errors, I believe that the information may be accepted as generally correct. In any case, it should help to give people a better understanding of the man who wrote the *Rules* and of the reasons back of his writing.

If it serves to bring General Robert into the view of his followers as a living, very human personality, and if it helps to show why his work has been found so acceptable by so many people, it will have served its purpose. We shall find the *Rules* less of a cold, impersonal structure, and a much more human document, made to help and not to confuse us, when we realize that their creator was a man puzzled as we are by the problems of procedure. He brought out of his own confusion an orderly, systematic method of working together.

A man's life story begins with his ancestors, as far back as possible, but certainly with his great-grandparents.

This is especially true of a man such as General Robert, whose strength of character and love of justice must have been a direct inheritance from his Huguenot ancestry. The little which we know about his forefathers confirms this theory.

America owes a debt of gratitude to the religious and social disturbances which arose in Europe during the seventeenth and eighteenth centuries. Conflicts, both political and religious, were a major influence in stimulating the desire to migrate to the New World where there were opportunities to escape from tyranny of the older civilization.

13

Men and women of sturdy character and unyielding conscience were driven from their homes by persecution. To these, primitive America beckoned with the promise of freedom. Many chose to make the perilous journey, assuming the role of pioneers in an unexplored land of untamed wilderness rather than surrendering their integrity. It was such people as these who laid the foundations of what we like to consider the typical American character.

The Huguenots, those deeply religious individualists from the south of France, were one of the groups influential in taming the American continent. They had survived a century of persecution without ever being shaken from their convictions. When Louis XIV, in 1685, revoked the Edict of Nantes, putting an end to the semblance of protection which had been granted them, they were forced into flight for their lives. France lost half a million of her sturdiest citizens in those distressful days. Some of these found a refuge in Switzerland and other parts of Europe, but many sought new homes in America, where freedom of thought and conscience could be had at the price of danger and hardship.

Between 1685 and 1690 there came to what is now South Carolina a number of Huguenot families who established a settlement in the Santee vicinity. Among these was one Pierre Robert, lately of St. Imier, Switzerland, who arrived in 1686. A devout Christian man, he became the first pastor of the colony, and continued as the spiritual leader for many years.

Pierre Robert was the several times great-grandfather of Henry Martyn Robert. The line of succession ran: Pierre, Pierre, Jacques, John, James Jehu, and Joseph Thomas, who was the father of the author of the *Rules of Order*. The characteristics of his ancestors had persisted through the generations, and this man too was a minister, even as his original American ancestor had been.

Joseph Thomas Robert was born November 28, 1807, in Beaufort District, South Carolina. He died March 5, 1884, having lived to see the good work of his distinguished son come to a point of general recognition. His own training had prepared him for a long life of service.

He was graduated from Brown University in 1828, and four years later from South Carolina Medical College, after having spent two years at Yale. This somewhat miscellaneous training led at last into the ministry. He was ordained in 1834 as the pastor of the Baptist Church of Robertsville, South Carolina.

He had been married in 1832 to Adeline Lawton, sister of General Alexander R. Lawton of Savannah, who was later to win fame during the War Between the States. Thus was brought about the union of two notable southern families, each with its record of patriotic service. Two ancestors, John Robert and Joseph Lawton, had been active in the days of the Revolution and had established honorable records in that conflict.

Henry Martyn Robert was born on May 2, 1837, on one of the family plantations near Robertsville, which was little more than a country crossroads with the store and church which served the people of the neighboring plantations. He came into a family with a background of character and education which might well be expected to produce a man of the highest type.

Detailed information is lacking on the early education of the young Robert, but we know that he entered West Point Military Academy in 1853, so it is safe to assume that a good grounding in the fundamentals enabled him to pass the entrance examinations. When he was graduated in 1857, it was with high honors. He held fourth rank in a class of thirty-eight young men.

In the meantime, his father had been making progress and winning recognition. In 1858, just a year after the West Point graduation, Dr. Joseph Robert was called to Burlington University in Burlington, Iowa, to teach mathematics and natural science. Five years later, the University of Iowa invited him to take the chair of languages. He remained in this post for several years, until Burlington University called him back to become its president.

In 1871 he returned to the South, as principal of the Augusta Institute for the training of Negro ministers, and in

1879 he was elected president of Atlanta Baptist Seminary, where he remained until the end of his life.

The young Henry Martyn Robert was a product worthy of this ancestry. With a background of scholarship and Christian character, he had a good start on a useful career, and he did not fail.

The story of this man's life might logically be divided into three sections. First, there was his profession as a military engineer in which he did notable work. Second, his service in the field of parliamentary law, which is the reason for our interest in him, deserves to have an entire book devoted to the study. Third, his life as a Christian citizen adds meaning to all his other works.

So closely are these three phases of his life interwoven that it is almost impossible to separate them in giving an account of his progress. Each is dependent on the other. Growth in all three phases was concurrent, and each contributed to the other.

Thus it has seemed wise, in this treatment of his life story, to carry the account as a whole, sacrificing logical division to the normal processes of growth and development, and presenting the picture of a man whose life was a gradual unfolding of talents awakened by the challenge of opportunity.

CHAPTER II

Constructing the Career

During his student days at West Point, the future General attracted the attention of his teachers by his exceptional ability in mathematics and related subjects. As a result, when only nineteen years of age he was called upon to act as assistant to the professor of mathematics, an assignment which he must have filled with efficiency. Following his graduation, he was appointed an assistant professor of practical military engineering, and, in addition, was given teaching duties in astronomy and natural philosophy. For so young a man this was a heavy responsibility, which may be taken as evidence of ability far above the ordinary.

A Special Order, dated at West Point Military Academy October 12, 1857, reads:

> "In accordance with Special Order No. 125 dated War Department, Adjutant General's Office, Washington, August 28, 1857, Bvt. 2nd Lieut. Henry M. Robert, Corps of Engineers, is assigned to duty in the Department of Practical Engineering, and will report to Lt. Donelson for such duties only as will not interfere with his labors in the Department of Nat. and Exp't. philosophy.
>
> By order of Major Delafield"

This order appeared to dispose of the matter of Lieutenant Robert's duty, but it proved to be only a temporary assignment. He was soon called to other tasks, far from the field of teaching.

Those were days of political turmoil, exploration, and

development in the United States, and so able a young man was not to be left for long in a quiet teaching position. Only a year after his graduation, he was called to more active service. He was ordered to the Washington Territory, which was then a comparatively unknown and almost completely unexplored region of the Pacific Northwest.

Second Lieutenant Robert was assigned to duty with a detachment of troops to take charge of engineering operations in a campaign against the Indians, who were causing trouble in the new territory. Thus, the young man was placed in a situation where his theoretical knowledge was to be put to most practical uses, and where his ability would be thoroughly tested.

Right at the start he faced the problem of getting to the new field of operations, a problem quite as great as the ones which were to be encountered after his arrival. Travel across the continent by land was by covered wagon or by horseback, a dangerous and time-consuming process. The alternative was to go to Panama by ship, cross the Isthmus by land, and then take ship again to finish the journey to the Northwest. This was the route followed by Lieutenant Robert and his men.

The trip across the Isthmus, through the tropical jungles, was a hazardous one. One of its principal dangers was the so-called Panama fever, to which the white man was especially susceptible. The young lieutenant used every available means to protect his men against this menace, and he succeeded in bringing them through safely, but he himself fell a victim to the disease. He recovered in time to carry on with his mission when the scene of his activities was reached.

For more than two years he continued in the work in the Washington Territory, helping to explore the route for a wagon road from Fort Dalles, Oregon, to Salt Lake City, and later heading a detachment which surveyed a military route from Vancouver to Puget Sound. These were tasks to call forth the best abilities of a young officer who was not yet twenty-three years of age, but he seems to have conducted himself well in all the work.

He was keenly aware of his responsibilities and of his

duty to the men under his command. He had a proper respect for the section of the Army of which his detachment was a part, and a consciousness of the need for friendly cooperation with other branches of the service.

His good judgment is reflected in an order, officially labeled Order No. 2, dated at Fort Vancouver, August 18, 1859, which read in part:

"I. Orders have been received placing this detachment on duty at San Juan Island in connection with fortifications there to be erected. It is the only time in the history of our army that Engineer Soldiers have had the charge of a work of this kind, and the reputation of the Company and Corps is at stake. The Commanding Officer hopes that every man will do his duty as he will have to rely greatly upon their assistance.

II. The Military Reputation of the Engineer Company has always been of the highest order. It is to be hoped that this Detachment will fulfill the expectations of all. But the attention of the Detachment is called to the following:

(1) A soldier must always stand attention when being addressed by or addressing an Officer, and salute.

(2) A soldier must always salute when meeting an officer, except when at work and not in charge of a party.

III. The Detachment will probably have greater responsibilities than normally fall to the lot of soldiers. It will be necessary for the Commanding Officer to place men on any duty independent of their rank, selecting the men in such a way as to conduce to the greatest possible efficiency of the Detachment.

IV. It is to be hoped that the men will work in harmony and cheerfully so as to be a model to those who may be jealous of their peculiar position in the army, and not by conceit or indiscreet remarks give rise to any unpleasant feelings between themselves and the troops of the line."

This order ends with an exhortation to the men "to do everything in their power to keep up the reputation of the Company on the frontiers where Engineer Soldiers have never been seen before."

His sense of fairness is shown in another order which is dated from Fort Cascadia, February 7, 1860. This order refers to a paragraph in an earlier order which ruled against any expression of opinion by members of the detachment who might be in disagreement with an officer. Lieutenant Robert was wise enough to realize that even a soldier of the line might have an idea which would help, and he was quick to revoke an instruction which prohibited a man from offering a suggestion. He wrote:

"So much of Detachment Order dated March 21st, 1859, as prohibited any member of the Detachment from offering his opinion to an officer is hereby revoked. It is proper and advisable that every man should express his mind wherever his hands are employed, and if he thinks that he could suggest some improvement, it is not the desire of the Commanding Officer to suppress such suggestion, provided it is made in a proper manner."

All these orders refer to an incident which, while almost forgotten today, was so serious at the time as to bring the United States and Great Britain almost to the point of war. The order sending the detachment of Engineers to San Juan Island "in connection with fortifications there to be erected" grew out of this situation.

The dispute over the boundary in the Northwest between Canada and the United States had not been fully settled, although a treaty adopted in 1846 had fixed the line of the 49th parallel as the official limit. As settlers moved into the territory, there was increasing dissension over certain points. Both sides claimed the Island of San Juan de Fuca, which lay on the boundary line, and the Americans were reluctant to give up their insistence on the slogan "Fifty-four forty or fight!"

As the controversy became hot, orders were issued to take possession of the island under dispute. The national capital at Washington, D.C. was many weeks away from the scene of trouble, so far as communications were concerned, and it took a long time for instructions and news to reach the officers in the field.

All United States troops in the region were ordered to San Juan Island, and Lieutenant Robert was placed in charge of the construction of defensive works to repel the expected attack.

It must have been a peculiar sort of military preparation in which these men engaged. The only artillery available consisted of eight 32-pounders taken from the transport Massachusetts, a very inadequate armament for the area involved; but fortifications were thrown together, the guns were placed to the best advantage, and all was made ready for the battle.

Fortunately, no clash occurred. General Winfield Scott appeared on the scene soon after the fortifications had been completed, and by his orders the troops were withdrawn, leaving the controversy for peaceable adjustment.

A little later Lieutenant Robert was recalled to Washington, D.C., where he was stationed when the War Between the States began. He was immediately called upon for service in defense work.

His first assignment was in the construction of the defense of the city of Washington. A little later he was transferred to Philadelphia for similar work. In 1862 he was transferred to New Bedford, Massachusetts, and placed in charge of construction work in that locality.

CHAPTER III

First Venture in Chairmanship

It may be wondered what connection there is between all these activities and the *Rules of Order*. The answer is that we had to bring the young officer to New Bedford in a logical manner, in order that we might arrive at the inception of his interest in parliamentary matters.

It was while he was stationed at New Bedford that he had his first encounter with the problems of chairmanship. This marked the beginning of the interest which later was to become a compelling force in his life.

One day he happened to attend a meeting of citizens of the community who were, presumably, preparing to engage in some service connected with the war effort. Some enthusiastic member of this group, probably inspired by the uniform and the impressive military bearing of Lieutenant Robert, nominated the officer for chairman of the meeting, and he was promptly elected.

This was his first venture in the field of chairmanship and, as usually happens in such a case, it was a distressing experience. Later in life he wrote of this incident: "The writer will never forget his embarrassment."

He found himself in the chair, with a meeting to be conducted, and with only the foggiest idea of what to do with it. Of course, he had attended meetings and had casually observed the conduct of presiding officers, but that was as far as it went. He knew that a chairman should have a gavel, with which he hammered the table at appropriate times, and that he should on occasion say, "All those in favor please say 'Aye'." But that was about the extent of his knowledge.

Such an embarrassing experience is likely to lead a man into either one of two courses of action. He may go from the meeting with a sense of failure, smarting under the consciousness of defeat, and vowing that he will never again get caught in such a predicament. This is the way that most of us react. On the other hand, he may decide if his way through life is to be attended by such hazards, he will prepare to meet them.

Fortunately for all of us, Lieutenant Robert chose the latter course. Since a working knowledge of parliamentary procedure appeared to be a necessary part of an officer's equipment, he made up his mind that he would acquire that knowledge. This decision started the train of events which culminated in the recognition of Henry Martyn Robert as America's highest authority on parliamentary law.

Studying parliamentary procedure in 1862 was a very different matter from such a study in our time. Today, the libraries have shelves well stocked with books treating every phase of chairmanship, and new publications are issued in a steady stream.

It is a significant fact that virtually all the books of this nature which have been produced in the last half century have been commentaries on the *Rules* devised by Robert rather than any new and improved methods which might replace his work. There is no lack of information and advice on the subject.

In the mid-nineteenth century there was no such abundance. Lieutenant Robert seems to have had an experience in his quest for information which is not unlike my own experience in searching for facts about his life and work. There was little to be found.

Two books seem to have constituted the entire list of current material. The *Manual of Parliamentary Practice* by Luther S. Cushing had been published in 1845. As the only popular work on the subject, it had won general acceptance. Aside from that, Jefferson's *Digest of the Rules of Congress* held a place of importance, due in large measure to the reputation of its author as a statesman. This work had served as a guide for most of the state legislatures and other legislative bodies, but it had not much to offer for the ordinary popular assemblies and organizations of non-political nature.

It appears that Lieutenant Robert did not have access to either of these books when he set out on his quest. Perhaps it is a good thing for us that he did not have them at the time, for they might have satisfied his immediate need, so that he would not have gone forward with his own studies, and his *Rules* might never have been compiled. Later on, when he did become acquainted with Cushing's *Manual*, his thinking on the subject had sufficiently matured to enable him to detect the illogical and unsatisfactory treatment of many procedural problems.

As it was, the only material which he could find in New Bedford was contained in a few pages on parliamentary law included in a *Compendium of Universal Knowledge*, a book which was a part of the furniture of many homes of those days. From this meager source he drew information which seemed to be sufficient to meet his immediate necessity.

Wondering at the scarcity of material on such an important subject, he made careful notes for his own guidance, and then counted the matter closed so far as he was concerned. Nothing was further from his mind at this time than the thought that he would ever have occasion to make exhaustive studies into the problems of parliamentary procedure.

One other incident of the years at New Bedford was the advancement of Lieutenant Robert to the rank of Captain, which marked another step in the series of promotions which eventually brought to him the title of Brigadier General.

At the close of the war, he was recalled to West Pont, where he was placed in charge of the Department of Practical Military Engineering, and was also made Treasurer of the institution. His stay at the Academy was of short duration, for in 1867, with his commission as Major, he was assigned to the staff of General Halleck, Commander of the Military Division of the Pacific. He remained in this assignment until 1871, serving under General Halleck's successors, General George H. Thomas and General J. M. Schofield.

During these years, he was in charge of lighthouse and

24

harbor construction on the west coast. With headquarters in San Francisco, he ranged up and down the coast, leaving the mark of his engineering genius on many important maritime works.

This assignment to duty on the Pacific Coast was another important step in his career as a parliamentarian, although he did not realize it at the time. In San Francisco he came into contact with people from all over the nation and from other lands, and his natural interest in human relations caused him to observe their differences in thought and practice on various matters.

California was then, as now, the rendezvous of people from all of the states. The prospect of adventure and of riches attracted men of all sorts and conditions. It was a place where diversity was far more prevalent than conformity to standards.

This lack of standards was much in evidence when people came together in meetings of any kind. Since there was no generally recognized standard of procedure, any group which assembled to transact business was likely to be thrown into confusion by disagreement on the proper way to conduct a meeting. Each member reflected the practices peculiar to the locality from which he had come, and the result usually was a state of chaos.

Major Robert became keenly conscious of the need for some standards which would be conducive to uniform practice. His orderly mind rebelled against the confused state of things as he observed them.

Like his father, he was a loyal church member and thus participated in many assemblies which dealt with church affairs. He was troubled by the difficulty of getting action in meetings of such groups. He felt the impulse to do something about it.

CHAPTER IV

The Beginning of The Rules

It was at this time that he began a careful study of Cushing's *Manual* and of the rules of Congress, hoping to find in these books a solution for his problem. He found, however, that these differed from each other and from the methods in common use. His analysis revealed the absence of accepted principles and the presence of many inconsistencies, both in practice and in the rules as formulated.

His thought on these matters led presently to the preparation of a little fifteen page manual for the guidance of himself and his friends in conducting the work of the deliberative, charitable, social, and civic organizations in which they were interested. This pamphlet may be regarded as the foundation upon which Major Robert's later work was constructed, and upon which procedures in American assemblies are based.

He had this pamphlet printed in 1869, at his own expense, for circulation among his friends and associates. On a copy of the pamphlet, which is to be seen in the Library of Congress, General Robert had written this notation: "San Francisco, Calif., 1869. Set up with my type & a few copies printed at Hd Qrs Mil. Division of the Pacific. HMR. Never completed."

Of interest to every student of parliamentary procedure are the words with which the subject was introduced in the pamphlet:

"1.   All business should be brought before the assembly by a motion of a member, or by the presentation of a communication to the assembly.

Exceptions: It is not usual to make a motion to *Receive the Reports of Committees* or *Communications* to the assembly; and in many other cases in the ordinary routine of business, the formality of a motion is dispensed with; but should any member object, a regular motion becomes necessary.

2. Before a member can make a motion or address the assembly on any question, it is necessary that he *obtain the floor*; that is, he must rise and address the Presiding Officer, who, if no one else has the floor, and there is no undebatable question before the assembly, will announce his name as having the floor.

When two or more rise at the same time, the Presiding Officer must decide who is entitled to the floor, which he does by announcing that member's name. When a member has obtained the floor, he cannot be put off from addressing the assembly, on the question before it; nor, when speaking, can he be interrupted by any other member rising and moving an adjournment, or for the orders of the day, or by making any other privileged motion of the same kind; it being a general rule, that a member in possession of the floor, or proceeding with his speech, cannot be taken down or interrupted, but by a call to order; and the question of order being decided, he is still to be heard through. A call for adjournment, or for the orders of the day, or for the question, by members in their seats, is not a motion; as no motion can be made, without rising and addressing the chair, and being called to by the presiding officer. Such calls for the question are themselves breaches of order, which though the

member who has risen may respect them, as
an expression of the impatience of the assembly at further debate, do not prevent him
from going on if he pleases."

This pamphlet met with immediate approval among those
to whom it was made available, who found it helpful in expediting business. This gave to Robert the idea, as he put it,
for "a very brief pocket manual, so cheap that every member
of a church or society could own a copy, and so arranged as
to enable one quickly to find when any particular motion
could be made."

During the years in San Francisco, he had time to give
thorough study to Cushing's *Manual* with the thought that
it might prove to be the kind of work which was needed for
popular use. He quickly discovered the weaknesses in this
book, both as to material and typography. No doubt one of
his principal disappointments had to do with the arrangement, for the *Manual* was not well set up, and it was not easy
for the reader quickly to find answers to his questions. When
Robert prepared his own book, one of his first considerations
was the matter of typography, which he designed for ready
reference and for emphatic presentation of the essential
points. He made free use of bold face type and of emphatic
separation of paragraphs by topics, thus making it more
convenient for consultation by the confused chairman.

But even more serious in his mind was the fact that the
methods enumerated by Cushing differed in many important
respects from the popularly accepted practices. He found a
lack of adherence to basic principle, resulting in ambiguities
in practical use and in contradiction of some of the formulated rules. His conclusion was that Cushing had overlooked many of the fundamentals, and that the system he
offered could never be satisfactory.

Equally disappointing was his study of the rules of Congress. Here he found many elements which were unsatisfactory in so far as application to the needs of popular assemblies was concerned. While such rules perhaps were

necessary in the case of a state or national legislature, they were much too undemocratic for the ordinary society or club which convenes to determine the will of its members and to make that will effective, not to enact legislation or to adopt partisan measures.

For example, the Congressional rule which permitted the shutting off of debate by a simple majority vote was particularly obnoxious to his sense of fairness. This attitude is reflected in the well known rule requiring a two-thirds majority for any action which limits the rights of individual members in an assembly. Both the rules of Congress and those promulgated by Cushing permitted the decision of such questions to be made by a majority vote.

But the demands of his duties as a military engineer prevented Robert from engaging in the exhaustive study which he saw would be necessary in any revision of procedure for popular use. During these years in San Francisco he added little except experience to what had been done on his manual. His work with organizations along the Pacific Coast, where he had excellent opportunity for observation, revealed still more clearly the confusion which existed. Certainly there was an intensification of his conviction that something ought to be done about it.

Following the years in San Francisco came a period of duty in Portland, Oregon, after which there was a transfer to the Middle West. The army records show that Major Robert was stationed in Milwaukee from 1873 to 1883, superintending lighthouse construction on the Great Lakes as well as river and harbor improvements along the Mississippi. Here the climatic conditions affected his work of planning and building.

During the long winters when outdoor work was restricted, he found more time to pursue his studies on the subject which had come to fill so large a place in his thought.

During these years in Milwaukee he worked at reviewing his observations, evaluating his conclusions, and classifying the principles which he had developed as essentials of correct procedure. In the absence of detailed information, we may assume that all the principles of organizational work received careful study.

Major Robert's training as an engineer came into full service when he applied himself to the task of designing a set of rules for practical use in the conduct of assemblies. Probably he approached this project in much the same way that he would have begun work on designing a lighthouse for some special and unusual location.

An engineer or an architect is careful about foundations. These must be substantial, to carry the loads which will be placed upon them. There must always be a dependable starting point on which the structure shall be erected.

Thus the designer goes down to bed rock, if he can locate it. He must have his "datum" — his point from which all levels are figured. The entire structure is built up in relation to this point. Stresses and strains are carefully figured so that the building, when completed, will stand up under any test which may be applied to it.

And then there was the background of army training, which gave him a better conception of the possibility of preparing a set of rules, for he was thoroughly familiar with the *Manual of Arms* and various military textbooks. The careful observer will note in the *Rules of Order* numerous matters which are reminiscent of the *Manual of Arms*, both in material and arrangement.

The long period of study and reflection had confirmed Major Robert in his determination of the fundamental principles. The "will of the assembly" was his guiding star. This was his "datum." He was fond of saying, "We are here to get at the will of the assembly. This is the only valid reason for holding a meeting, and that must be the basis of all parliamentary action. That is our starting point."

Thus the engineer set to work to take apart the whole fabric of parliamentary law that he might reconstruct it on more logical and systematic lines. He analyzed the elements and studied their relationships from all points of view. He sought to determine the relative importance of the various actions as they concerned each other and the fundamental

30

"will of the assembly." He tried to complete this work of analysis before he began the construction. By this process he was ready to reassemble the elements in orderly fashion upon the foundation which he had established.

His attitude of mind is shown in a paragraph in the preface to the first edition of the *Rules,* where he states: "The object of rules of order is to assist an assembly to accomplish the work for which it was destined, in the best possible manner. To do this it is necessary to restrain the individual somewhat, as the right of the individual in any community to do what he pleases is incompatible with the interest of the whole."

And so he developed the several principles that the majority must rule, that the minority must be heard, that the rights of individuals must be guarded, and that justice and courtesy must prevail. He was firmly opposed to any of the "steam-roller" tactics so often used in political gatherings, and one may safely assume that he would have frowned upon the delaying and obstructive tricks which are sometimes employed in meetings. Probably he did not realize then, as he must have realized later, the fact that his carefully made rules could be utilized by obstructionists to interfere with the accomplishment of proper purposes.

Throughout the *Rules* we find evidence of Major Robert's sense of fairness. It is manifested at many points where meticulous care is given to methods for securing full hearing and free voting for all.

With his fundamental principles determined and always before him, he undertook to test each step of procedure. He sought to discover the basic relationships between the several steps involved in the introduction and consideration of business, and then he arranged the processes in harmony with the relationships. Such matters as the precedence of motions, the regulation of discussion, and the preservation of voting rights were arranged on the basis of relative importance and necessity.

Thus, in the hands of Major Robert, the whole scheme of parliamentary action was reduced to a consistent, logical, scientific structure. I am strongly inclined to add "for the first time," because while procedures had grown up through centuries of experience in the early town meetings and parliaments and tribal gatherings, so far as I can learn there had not been, before the days of Robert, any such attempt to systematize and codify the rules of conduct.

Major Robert engaged in a pioneer work comparable to that of his Huguenot ancestors who had come to the New World two centuries earlier to build a new home out of the raw materials they found in the wilderness. It was a new treatment of an old problem.

It takes time for an idea to germinate and grow into maturity; and it takes time for a great structure to be built. Robert, the engineer, had learned patience in his profession, and he needed this patience in his avocation as a parliamentarian.

His interest in the subject was of slow growth. He was twenty-six years of age when parliamentary procedure first became a personal interest to him in the experience in chairmanship at New Bedford. He was well past thirty before he undertook any serious study of the problem, and he was thirty-eight when the day came for the publication of his *Rules*. His great idea took time for its development, as is usually the case with many great ideas.

The casual student of parliamentary law who becomes confused as he tries to understand why a motion to lay on the table takes precedence over a motion to postpone, or why it requires a two-thirds vote to carry one kind of motion while another prevails by a simple majority, or why some motions must be seconded and others get along without seconds, should be able to sympathize with the man who faced the whole dizzy mass of procedure and undertook to untangle it and rearrange it in an orderly and comprehensible fashion. It was a task of herculean proportions. It called for the mind of an engineer, a logician, a mathematician, a philosopher, and an idealist, together with the patience of a plodding pilgrim, to construct the convenient system with which we are familiar.

It takes a fair degree of intelligence to understand and use the system which Robert created. Much more did it require an exceptional intellect to devise that system. Someone has unintentionally described the ability of this man in the words: "Genius is not a single power, but a combination of great powers."

"Part I," as we know it, was all that Robert had in mind when he began the work. It was his intention to set forth the principles on which parliamentary procedure should be based, and to let it go at that. Probably he intended simply to expand what he had done in his pamphlet *Manual* in San Francisco. The full extent of the completed work as we now have it had not yet entered his mind. The idea grew as he worked on it.

Months of most careful and painstaking study went into the preparation of his material and its arrangement for publication. While carrying a full load of responsibility in his profession, he still found time to devote to his hobby, if we may so term this compelling interest. There was no question in his own mind as to the value of what he was doing. He put his best into it, as was his custom with every duty. Even so, he had no conception of what would come of his efforts and of the influence that his book might have when finally brought to publication.

As we look through the book, we are repeatedly impressed by the manner in which his methodical thinking is manifested. We can see that his conclusions were formulated with keen discrimination. No detail was too small for his consideration; no problem was too hard for him to attack. Every step was taken with the watchful care of the engineer, making certain that each member of his structure was firmly anchored to its supports.

We who enjoy the benefits of his work can never fully appreciate the countless hours of study, the continual facing of choices and decisions, and the conscientious devotion with which every item was scrutinized.

The work was brought approximately to completion in 1874, and Major Robert faced the problem of finding a pub-

33

lisher. He then experienced the same trouble that many ambitious but unknown writers have had.

He sent the manuscript to D. Appleton and Company, of New York, and they missed a wonderful opportunity by politely declining to use it. Among the papers left by General Robert is a letter dated May 1, 1874, and written in longhand on the Appleton Company's letterhead. It reads:

"We return your Ms, as requested; our engagements are such that we cannot undertake its publication."

In later years they had reason to regret the sending of that letter, but they seem to have shared the two common mistakes of the time; first, that Cushing's *Manual* was sufficient, and second, that no one was interested in parliamentary procedure. How wrong they were on both counts!

In the meantime, the Major had written an article on "Parliamentary Law" for *The American Encyclopedia,* and there is a letter from the publishers, dated April 13, 1875, telling him that his article was to appear in the forthcoming edition of their work.

CHAPTER V

Publication at Last

It took more than the rejection by a publisher to discourage Major Robert. He knew what he had done, and he was convinced that the public needed and wanted it. So strong was his belief that he was willing to gamble on it. He was ready to back it with his own money.

Long before, he had decided in his own mind on the kind of book that he wished to give to the public. He planned to make it of convenient size to carry in one's pocket, easy to read, clearly divided into sections, and closely indexed for quick reference. It was to be a pocket-piece, a constant companion for the serious minded chairman. Robert wanted no massive quarto volume, to be left on library tables along with the dictionary and other seldom used works of reference.

The result of his planning was the handy little brown volume with which we are familiar, whose form, size, and color remained unchanged through so many years. The form and size are still the same, except for the thickening caused by added pages, but some recent editions have brought changes in the color of the binding.

Undaunted by the lack of enthusiasm on the part of publishers, Major Robert went ahead on his own account. He employed the firm of Burdick and Armitage, printers, of Milwaukee, to put his book into type. He selected the type faces and dictated the process of making up and arranging. He bought a supply of book paper of quality which met his specifications, and he helped the firm to buy new fonts of type to satisfy his requirements. The printers gave good cooperation and were able to comply with the wishes of their exacting customer.

The production of the material was a process quite different from the printing procedures of today. Type was set by hand, and then thrown down after being used. There were no stereotypes nor electrotypes. The printers had a press capable of handling only sixteen pages at a time, and so they purchased only type enough to set up that limited amount of copy.

When this frame of sixteen pages had been set up, proof sheets were taken off for correction. Because of the pressure of his duties, Major Robert was frequently unable to do the proofreading promptly, but when he had made the necessary corrections, the complete printing of four thousand copies was made from this frame. Then the type was distributed and the setting of the next sixteen pages was started. This meant that every frame, with cross references to the paging in the final form, must be absolutely perfect in all details before the type could be distributed. This laborious process took most of the year 1875.

Thus it appears that the printing of the book was almost as difficult and laborious a task as the writing of the material.

It must have been a proud day for him when he held in his hands the final proofs of his book and for the first time was able to think of it as a task completed. Wise man that he was, and recognizing the value of friendly criticism, the Major submitted these first proofs to his wife for suggestions and, possibly, for her approval. She gave him a frank opinion, which was just what he needed.

Mrs. Robert offered a suggestion for which we should all be grateful. Not questioning the wisdom and accuracy of his treatment of parliamentary matters, she recommended that something be added in the way of practical illustrations of the application of the principles. She sympathized with the ordinary, inexperienced reader who would try to grasp the complexities of procedure, and she suggested the addition of examples of how the rules would work.

Recognizing the reasonableness of this comment, Major

Robert immediately went to work on a new section of the book, presenting practical illustrations of the application of his principles to the conduct of a meeting. This became "Part Two," which most of us have found valuable in meeting our problems. We who use the *Rules* owe a debt of gratitude to Mrs. Robert for her timely suggestion. She was speaking for all of us when she asked for simplification and concreteness, and her commonsense criticism produced results which have been helpful to all.

With this new section completed, work went forward on the printing, but before it was done another factor intervened. Major Robert was a member of the Baptist Church, and he included its activities among his personal interests. In a church convention certain controversial matters came up. There was a question about the seating of delegates, and the decision had to be made as to who were proper members of the convention.

Out of this controversy grew the section of the book which deals with the right of an assembly to protect its own interests.

Remembering that this was the first printing of the book, and that there was nothing to guide the author except his own studies and observations, one must be impressed with his wisdom in both the selection and the presentation of the material; and one cannot overlook the depth of his wisdom as shown in the ready acceptance of the suggestions offered by his wife.

The general plan of the work is set forth in the "Introduction" to the early editions. I quote from the printing of 1882, where the author explains, under the heading "Plan of the Work":

"The manual is divided into three distinct parts, each complete in itself, and a Table of Rules containing a large amount of information in a tabular form, for easy reference in the midst of the business of a meeting. (Thus Major Robert anticipated the charts, tables, and diagrams which have engaged the attention of hundreds of teachers and writers since his time.)

"Part I contains a set of Rules of Order systematically arranged. . . . Each one of the forty-five sections is complete in itself, so that one unfamiliar with the work cannot be misled in examining any particular subject. . . .

"Part II is a Parliamentary Primer, giving very simple illustrations of the methods of organizing and conducting different kinds of meetings, stating the very words used by the chairman and speakers in making and putting various motions; . . . it also gives, briefly, the duties of the officers, forms of minutes, and reports of the treasurer and committees; it classifies the motions into eight classes according to their object, and then takes up separately each class and compares those in it, showing under what circumstances each motion should be used.

"Part III consists of a few pages devoted to miscellaneous matters that should be understood by members of deliberative assemblies, such as the important but commonly misunderstood subjects of the Legal Rights of Deliberative Assemblies and Ecclesiastical Tribunals, etc."

Thus the book developed, growing in size and scope with the demands put upon its author, and with his continuous observation of the needs which it must meet. It was a very human document, coming as it did out of personal experience. Perhaps the realization of this fact will help to relieve some of the dryness and apparent austerity of the material as it is read.

It was representative, too, for its growth covered the nation. Beginning with the New Bedford incident, back in 1863, Robert had carried his ideas across the continent and back again. Developed in San Francisco and tested in many localities, the material was brought at last to Milwaukee for complete study and refinement. If any man had the right, through wide experience, to set up standards for America to adopt, surely this was the man. His work was not something thought out in a laboratory, secluded from human contacts, but a document compiled from the daily life of men.

The printing went forward, and in due course four thousand copies of the book were done, complete except for the binding. Then Major Robert went to Chicago to talk with a publisher, for he fully realized the necessity, for the sake of prestige, of having the book issued over the name of some well known and reputable publishing house.

On the day late in 1875 when he entered the office of S. C. Griggs and Company, Chicago publishers, no one realized that the dignified officer carried a potential gold mine in the parcel under his arm. He met with a cool reception on the part of the publishers who were extremely reluctant to assume the responsibility for introducing a new book by an unknown author on a comparatively unpopular subject.

"It is quite useless," said the head of the firm, "to accept a book on parliamentary law from an unknown writer, for Cushing and parliamentary law are synonymous terms. Moreover, what in the world can an army officer know about parliamentary law?"

The determined author resolutely stood his ground. He knew his work, and he was ready to support it. He had already put a substantial sum of his own money into the printing. He was willing to invest more.

He must have presented a powerful argument. He carefully explained that he was trying to substitute for the illogical procedures of the day a thoroughly logical scheme which would standardize practice throughout the nation, and win acceptance because of its simplicity and commonsense methods. He was confident that his work would win because of its intrinsic merit. His own experience had proved to him that it was sorely needed. As evidence of his faith in it, he made a proposition which the publisher could hardly afford to turn down.

Major Robert proposed to use for advertising purposes one thousand of the four thousand copies which had been printed. If the Griggs Company would proceed with the binding and publication, he would take the first thousand books and send them at his own expense to people who ought to be competent to judge the value of what he had done. He listed officers of legislatures, editors, legal authorities, college professors, and presidents of fraternal and religious bodies to whom the book would be sent, with the request for frank criticism. It was a daring publicity scheme for that day, but it promised to give promptly an honest sampling of the popular reaction while at the same time it would furnish wonderful publicity for the book.

Robert was certain in his own mind that the United States needed such a guide, and he believed that his work was more truly in accord with the American spirit than any other writing on the subject. If he was right, the critics would favor the book and welcome it gladly, while if he was mistaken, condemnation would properly and surely result. Thus he would find out whether he had done something distinctly worth while, or had just written another book. If it failed, he would be the loser.

Faced with such a proposal, the publishers finally capitulated and agreed to handle the matter as he requested. With one thousand copies sold at the start and with only three thousand left on their hands, their risk was not great, and they took it. Major Robert turned over to them for binding his stock of printed copies.

In the original contract with the S. C. Griggs Company, dated January 20, 1876, the full title of the book was given as: *Pocket Manual of Rules of Order for Deliberative Assemblies*. This contract, in Major Robert's own handwriting, provided for him to pay the Griggs Company twelve cents per copy for binding the books.

Before the official publication date, Major Robert had proceeded with his publicity plan, sending out copies of the book to many persons and publications for comment. Thus it happened that on February 19, 1876, the day when the little *Manual* was offered to the public, notices began to appear in newspapers concerning it.

The Chicago *Inter-Ocean* of February 19th carried words of commendation, including the following paragraph:

"It has been well remarked by a great writer on English Parliamentary Law that it is much more material that there should be a rule to go by than what that rule is. Uniformity in procedure is really what is wanted among deliberative bodies."

The Chicago *Standard* published a complimentary review on February 24th, in which it was said:

"A book more needed has not appeared in many a day. We are happy to find that this one meets the case so admirably."

The newspaper notices generally called it "a convenient, complete, thin little book, well printed on fine paper, with remarkably clear type, well arranged, and with cross references well made."

In a scrapbook kept by Major Robert there is a collection of these press notices, gathered from newspapers and magazines all over the nation, and almost without exception giving high praise. To show the wide spread of interest, we take note of some of these early comments as to source.

The Memphis *Daily Advocate* told the story on March 5, 1876. The Salt Lake *Daily Times* followed suit on March 25, 1876, and on April 13 the Alabama *Baptist* recommended the book.

The *Argus,* Rock Island, Illinois, presented the story in its issue of May 6, the Milwaukee *Sentinel* on May 12, and the *New England Farmer*, of Boston, on June 17.

In March 1876, the *College Courier*, published by Monmouth College at Monmouth, Illinois, offered this comment:

"We have just received a copy of 'Rules of Order,' a neat little work of 175 pages. It is highly recommended by parliamentarians and is just the book to supply the long felt want of our literary societies. Robert's Manual cannot be excelled for simple, convenient and comprehensive treatment of the subject."

With such a wave of favorable publicity, it is not surprising that the stock of books was quickly depleted. Orders flowed in, and books were shipped out. Within three months the surprised publishers were contemplating empty shelves, while orders piled up which they could not fill. They had to admit that Major Robert was right. They went promptly to work printing more books.

The Chicago *Daily Journal* of May 20th carried a display advertisement from the S. C. Griggs Company, announcing completion of the fifth thousand of the books printed since February. In the meantime they had called upon the author for revisions and added material which he considered desirable. The demand continued to outrun the supply, and the presses were kept rolling to provide more copies of the *Rules*.

Commendations continued to be published by periodicals, each contributing in some measure to the sale. On December 16, 1876, *The Church Union*, published in New York, said:

"Upon opening this little book, we at once rejoice in its numerous commendable features — a thoroughly refined plan, and the last degree of brevity. It is by far the best of its kind we have ever seen."

A most interesting note is sounded in the Chicago *Standard* of June 21, 1877, when the book had been in circulation for sixteen months:

"This remarkably convenient parliamentary guide seems to be rapidly gaining ground. It has just been adopted as the standard authority of the United Presbyterian Church."

There was prompt recognition for the value of a detailed, logical, practical plan for expediting procedure in ordinary meetings. Apparently there was a general acceptance of the sentiment expressed by one English writer on parliamentary law who wrote:

"Whether these forms be in all cases the most rational or not is really not of so great importance. It is much more material that there should be a rule to go by than what that rule is, so that there may be uniformity of proceeding in business, not subject to the caprice of the chairman or captiousness of the members. It is very material that order, decency, and regularity be preserved in a dignified public body."

Robert's *Rules* clearly met this requirement by providing an orderly method of procedure simple enough to be used by anyone, and yet comprehensive enough to meet all needs. Whether or not the plan was absolutely the best in every particular that could be produced, it was conceded to be the best that had thus far been produced, and it did provide that basis for uniform practice which had long been needed.

In the early editions, the publishers printed on the fly leaves testimonials from some of the prominent people who had studied and used the book. Some of these comments are worth repeating here:

Lieutenant-Governor J. M. Bingham, President of the Wisconsin State Senate in 1881, wrote: "I used it constantly during the recent session of the Senate, and was always able to find the point I was called upon to decide. It is invaluable to a presiding officer."

The Hon. W. H. Parks, Speaker of the Assembly of the State of California at its twenty-fourth session, said: "I have been using Robert's Rules of Order and I consider it an excellent arrangement of the rules of parliamentary law.'

There is a glowing tribute from Carter H. Harrison, Mayor of the City of Chicago, who pronounced the book the best he had seen, and stated his opinion that it ought to govern all deliberative bodies. Strong words of commendation were quoted from General Albert Pike, 33rd Degree Most Potent Sovereign, Grand Commander of the Supreme Council of 33rd Degree Ancient and Accepted Scottish Rite of Free Masonry, Southern Jurisdiction of the United States.

From W. M. Bennett, Past Grand Master of the Ancient Order of United Workers of the State of New York, came a statement that he had secured the adoption of Robert's *Rules of Order* as standard both for local lodges and the Supreme Lodge of his order.

J. M. Stone of Mississippi testified: "For general use I think it is superior to any work I have examined."

In addition to the personal endorsements of many such

43

notables, there was printed a paragraph setting forth the fact that the *Rules* were the accepted parliamentary standard throughout many states in the work of the Odd Fellows, the Knights of Pythias, the Grand Army of the Republic, the Ancient Order of United Workmen, and others, as well as in hundreds of college societies, debating clubs and similar organizations.

Since these statements were published within five or six years after the initial appearance of the book, it is evident that the new work won popular favor with a speed which was nothing less than phenomenal for that day. There must have been a definite need, and Robert's *Rules* must have met that need.

Because of its practical utility, it gained this wide acceptance, starting Major Robert on the course which justifies our title for him, "The Great Peacemaker." By 1890 it had become the custom for organizations to write into their by-laws the clause making *Robert's Rules of Order* the final authority on all points of procedure not specifically covered in the rules of the society. And it is safe to say that three-fourths of the people who followed his *Rules* never awoke to the fact that his name was not "Roberts" but "Robert."

The quality of the work is attested by the fact that no other book on the subject has superseded this one, despite the lapse of years. Countless books on parliamentary practice have been written, but almost without exception they have been commentaries on the work of Robert rather than original contributions to the subject. Robert's *Rules* still order us.

The popularity of the *Rules* quickly raised Major Robert to prominence as an authority on parliamentary matters and brought him many invitations to lecture, some of which he was able to accept without prejudice to his army work. People developed the habit of writing to him for rulings on points which were not understood. He tried faithfully to reply to these, in so far as possible, and his correspondence grew to formidable proportions. Many of the inquiries came from women's organizations.

Here is a sample of such questions and answers, in a letter addressed to Mrs. John C. Hazen, Pelham Manor, New York.

"Dear Madam:—

Yours of the 25th ultimo arrived during my absence in New Orleans. Your questions I repeat with my answers following.

1. *Query:* Is any one at liberty to see the minutes of any meeting before these minutes have been read and accepted at the regular monthly meeting?

    Answer: No, except the Presiding Officer.

2. *Query:* Should the Secretary ever allow her minutes to go out of her possession and run the risk of their being lost or not returned?

    Answer: The Secretary is responsible as custodian of the records. She may, if she sees fit, allow a responsible member to take the minutes and examine them. In doing this, however, the Secretary is responsible for any mutilation of the records resulting from her act."

Another letter is addressed to Mr. G. Edmonston, Washington, D.C., which reads as follows:

"Dear Sir:—

In reply to yours of the 21st instant I would say that when an amendment of a resolution is pending no other amendment of the resolution is in order. After the first amendment has been disposed of, then it is in order to offer a second amendment, and so on without limit.

You will find this in Rules of Order, Section 23, which says that to amend "takes precedence of nothing but the question which it is proposed to amend." On page 18, you will find the definition of the expression "takes precedence" from which you will see that as to amend takes precedence of nothing but the motion to be amended, it can only be moved on the last pending question. Thus if an amendment is pending you can amend nothing but the amendment; if the motion to refer is pending you can amend only the motion to refer as it is the only motion it takes precedence of, and so on."

From the samples it is evident that people of sixty or seventy years ago were troubled by the same questions that we meet today, and that instead of searching out the answers for themselves, they used the easier method of writing to the authority.

Many interesting and sometimes amusing experiences occurred in connection with the lecturing and instructing and writing of letters in reply to perplexed inquirers.

There is one incident dating from the days when Robert lived in Milwaukee which serves to illustrate the reputation he had won even at that early time. A Chicago man, visiting the office of the S. C. Griggs Company, remarked that he would very much like to see Major Robert in action, conducting a meeting.

Mr. Griggs suggested that Major Robert was to preside at a large church convention in Milwaukee, and that the gentleman might do well to attend as an observer.

A few days later, Mr. Griggs met the man again and asked, "Did you go up to Milwaukee to see Robert preside?"

"Yes, I did," was the answer, in a rather disgusted tone.

"What's the matter?" asked Mr. Griggs. "Didn't things go smoothly?"

"Yes," said the other. "I went all the way to Milwaukee to see how this man Robert would get himself out of a jam. The whole thing went so smoothly that there was just nothing to see."

Another document, unfortunately without a date, reflects the keen interest of Robert in his church affairs. He was called upon frequently to pass judgment on some problem which arose from the business of organizations in the church, and his advice seems always to have been clear, consistent, and well considered.

Here are a few paragraphs from his writing on the need for decorum in procedure in religious organizations:

"Members of Baptist churches are constantly called upon to perform the duties devolving upon members of deliberative assemblies. Our organization is such that the local church is the highest body we recognize, and consequently may at any time have the most delicate duties to perform. The necessity for some system and order in its deliberations seems so apparent that it can hardly be conceived that one would deny it. As long as there are differences of opinion, so long will there be need for rules and laws.

"The fact that the assembly is composed only of Christians does not affect the case. One can scarcely have had much experience in deliberative meetings of Christians without realizing that the best of men, having wills of their own, are liable to attempt to carry out their own views without paying respect to the rights of their opponents. As much as we may oppose the theory that "the end justifies the means," human nature is such that under the excitement of debate, most enthusiastic persons lose sight of everything but the one object they are seeking to accomplish. The writer has seen one of the ablest ministers in our denomination rule out of order a motion to adjourn, because he was so opposed to it that he felt it *ought* to be out of order. But even supposing that Christian people never get excited, there must be some forms of proceeding for their business meetings, and every meeting has some forms and rules, whether they know it or not. Some motions are, and some are not, in order during debate of another question. Some questions can be amended and some cannot, and some questions are debatable and some undebatable.

"The possibility of being out of order pre-supposes

some system of order which one may violate. One cannot be "out of order" without there is a rule of order to which he should conform. The most terrible tyranny is that of the mob that pretends to recognize no law, and therefore becomes of necessity the slave of its own passion and submits to the worst of all laws: "Might makes right."

"The next worst form of government is where the law is entirely dependent upon the will of him who executes it, and that executive office is continually changing. If the Dictator is permanent, his acts soon form a body of precedent by which his future action can be calculated, but where he is constantly changing, as has been the case at some time in the history of most of the great nations of antiquity, then no one can form an idea of the law.

"In most of our religious deliberative meetings, no one knows the laws that govern them. The presiding officer of that particular meeting makes the law which is to apply to each case after the action has occurred to which the law is to apply. Experience has taught us that to preserve individual rights it is best to have definite written laws, and made so public that each one can, if he wishes, know the laws he is required to obey.

"The experience in deliberative assemblies has been the same. True freedom requires that we know the laws to which we must submit, and that those laws be as definite as possible, and not subject to be changed at the caprice of anyone. Good laws are a benefit to the well-disposed, and only a hindrance to those who would do evil."

That statement of principles seems to apply equally well to the affairs of any organization or government. The selection from this writing by Robert deserves careful reading and reflection by all citizens.

There is another statement which should be included. It is an extract from a letter which is undated, but which was

Photo by courtesy of Corps of Engineers, U. S. Army,
Office of Galveston District.

A section of the original Galveston Seawall, completed in 1904. Note the concave face of the wall, designed to break the force of storm driven waves; and the piles of riprap which anchor the base of the structure.

The monument in the foreground, a twin of the one which commemorates the committee of engineers, gives dates of construction of the Seawall, the Seawall Boulevard, and the sidewalk, with the dates for the work; and it lists the names of county officials who were active in the project.

Here are seen Luther H. Evans, former Librarian of Congress, and Mrs. Isabel Hoagland Robert, discussing some of the materials in the memorial exhibit. Mrs. Robert gave invaluable help in making available much of the material presented in this book.

This picture was made in 1921, about two years before the death of General Robert. Note the firmness of his signature.

On August 27, 1954, a company of Toastmasters who were attending the great Convention of Toastmasters International, joined in a pilgrimage to the tomb of General Henry Martyn Robert, in Arlington National Cemetery. In the picture are seen, from the left, Henry Martyn Robert III, grandson of the great parliamentarian, Russell V. Puzey, President of Toastmasters, Mrs. Sarah Corbin Robert, widow of Henry Martyn Robert II, and Ralph C. Smedley, who delivered a brief euology in placing a wreath on the tomb.

Brigadier General Henry Martyn Robert, Chief of Engineers, U. S. Army, taken at the time of his retirement from active service in 1901.

This is the only known photograph of Henry Martyn Robert before he entered West Point in 1853. It is reproduced from an old daguerreotype.

Photograph by courtesy of Library of Congress

On the 75th anniversary of the publication of Robert's Rules of Order, observed on February 19, 1951, the Library of Congress placed on view an exhibit pertaining to the work and its distinguished author, General Henry Martyn Robert. From the left, in the picture, are seen Mrs. Henry Martyn Robert, Jr., Isabel Hoagland Robert, widow of General Robert, Mrs. De-Witt Clinton Redgrave, General Robert's daughter, and Luther E. Evans, former Librarian of Congress.

The square granite monument stands on the top of the Galveston
Seawall, and shows the names of county and city officers who directed the construction of the flood protective works. On the side
shown in the picture appear the names of General Henry Martyn
Robert, Alfred Noble and H. C. Ripley, the engineers who designed
the project.

D. APPLETON & CO.

549 & 551 BROADWAY.

BOOKSELLERS, PUBLISHERS AND STATIONERS.

New York, May 1, 1874

Maj. Robert

    Dr Sir

    We return your Ms. as requested, Our engagements are such that we cannot under-take its publication—

    Yours

    D. Appleton & Co.

D. Appleton & Company missed a great opportunity when they returned the manuscript of the *Rules of Order*, with this letter, dated May 1, 1874.

Head Quarters, Military Academy,
West Point N.Y. October 12, 1857

Special Orders
No. 147

In accordance with Special Orders No 125,
dated War Department, Adjutant Generals Office, Washington,
August 28, 1857. Bvt. 2d Lieut. Henry M. Robert Corps of Engineers,
is assigned to duty in the Department of Practical Engineering
& will report to St. Donelson, for such duties only as will not interfere
with his labors in the Department of Nat. & Exp.l Philosophy

By order of Major Delafield
James B. Fry
1st Lieut. 1st Arty.
Adjutant M. A.

Army Order, dated October 12, 1857, assigning Lieutenant Robert
to duties in addition to the work as an instructor in the Department
of Nat. & Expt. Philosophy at West Point.

Fort Cascades, W.T. Feby 7th 1860

Orders }
No }

    I. The Detachment Order dated "Fort Cascades W.T. December 18th 1858" appointing Corpl McEnany Acting Sergeant of Engineers is hereby revoked.

    II. So much of Detachment Order dated "Fort Cascades W.T. March 21st 1859" as prohibits any member of the detachment from offering his opinion to an officer, is hereby revoked. It is proper & advisable that every man should exercise his mind wherever his hands are employed & if he thinks that he could suggest some improvement either it is not the desire of the Comdg officer to suppress such suggestions provided it is made in a proper manner.

    III. The attention of the Detachment is called to the remainder of the last mentioned order. It is to be hoped that this will be sufficient to prevent any more breaches of discipline as far as Saluting is Concerned.

            Henry M Robert
            2nd Lieut Engineers

This order, dated February 7, 1860, is of great interest as reflecting the fundamental fairness of Lieutenant Robert. Revoking a former order which prohibited members of the Detachment under his command from offering suggestions, the young officer invited the men to help with their ideas; rather an advanced position for a commanding officer to take in that day.

Samples selected from the correspondence of General Robert to show his care in replying to inquiries on matters of parliamentary procedure. Such letters came in great numbers, and everyone was answered with care, so far as time permitted.

In more recent years, such a correspondence has been carried on by Henry Martyn Robert, Jr., and by Mrs. Sarah Corbin Robert, since the death of her husband.

SUBJECT: Parliamentary Law.

Colonel HENRY M. ROBERT,
Corps of Engineers, U. S. Army.

ENGINEER OFFICE,
U. S. ARMY.

ARMY BUILDING, 39 WHITEHALL STREET,

NEW YORK CITY,

March 4, 1901.

Mrs. John C. Hazen,

Pelham Manor, N.Y.

My Dear Madam:

Yours of the 25th ultimo arrived during my absence in New Orleans. Your questions I repeat with my answers following.

1. Query: Is any one at liberty to see the minutes of any meeting before these minutes have been read and accepted at the regular monthly meeting?

Answer: No, except the Presiding Officer.

2. Query: Should the Secretary ever allow her minutes to go out of her possession and run the risk of their being lost or not returned?

Answer: The Secretary is responsible as custodian of the records. She may, if she sees fit, allow a responsible member to take the minutes and examine them. In doing this, however, the Secretary is responsible for any mutilation of the records resulting from her act.

Trusting that these answers are sufficiently clear, I am

Very truly yours,

Henry M Robert

Colonel HENRY M. ROBERT,
Corps of Engineers, U. S. Army.

ENGINEER OFFICE,
U. S. ARMY.

ARMY BUILDING, 39 WHITEHALL STREET,

NEW YORK CITY,

September 29,1900.

Mrs. Alice M. Heper,

840 Washington Boulevard,

Chicago, Ill.

Dear Madam:

Yours without date is at hand. The question which you submit is, as I understand it, as follows:

An incorporate society has by-laws which give no special power to the Directors, their duty being described as "they shall have the management of the business of the club and shall fill all vacancies": can such a Board of Directors suspend or amend a by-law formally adopted by the Club?

The answer to such a question of course is <u>no</u>. The Directors have no more power over the By-laws and Constitution of the organization, unless such power is given them specifically in said instruments, than the United States Congress has over the Constitution of the United States.

Sometimes the by-laws of a society give to the Board of Directors the power to modify,or, in some cases even, to make the by-laws of a society, but in the case which you refer to me, the society has not given such power, and the Board of Directors has no power except what is specifically given it.

I think this answers your question.

Very truly yours,

Henry M. Robert

SUBJECT: Rules of Order.

Lieut. Col. HENRY M. ROBERT,
Corps of Engineers, U.S.A.

ENGINEER OFFICE, U. S. ARMY,

ROOM H 7, ARMY BUILDING, 39 WHITEHALL STREET.

New York, N. Y., January 25th,   189 4.

Mr. Edgar S. Werner,

    108 East 16th Street,

        New York City.

Dear Sir:

        In reply to yours of the 17th instant, forwarded to my present
address, I would say that the appointment of a nominating committee is
designed to take the place of open nominations, but after the committee
has reported a member could ask unanimous consent to his making a nomination, or I suppose, the chair would usually recognize a motion to permit
another nomination, though he should be careful not to allow this privilege to be used to obstruct business. In other words, the presumption
is that the society appointed the nominating committee to avoid open nominations. Yet it is possible that it may not object to the formal nomination of an opposition ticket, if too much time is not lost thereby.
This open nomination, however, under such circumstances is not a right but
a privilege granted by unanimous consent or a formal vote.

        Very respectfully yours,

        Henry M Robert

        Lieut. Col., Corps of Engineers.

THE STATE OF TEXAS

COUNTY AND CITY OF GALVESTON

     This Memorandum made in duplicate this 5th. day of December A. D. 1901, WITNESSETH:

     I. That under provision and authority of the Charter of the City of Galveston, the Board of Commissioners of said City have appointed Gen. H.M. Robert, United States, A. retired, Mr. Alfred Noble of Chicago, and Maj. H.C. Ripley formerly of Galveston to be and constitute a Board of Engineers to devise and report to said Board of Commissioners plans and specifications with estimates of the cost:

     1st. For the safest and most efficient way for protecting said City against overflows from the sea:

     2nd. For elevating filling and grading the avenues, streets, sidewalks, alleys and lots of said City, so as to protect said City from overflow from the waters of the Gulf and to secure sufficient elevation for drainage and sewerage.

     3rd. For a breakwater or seawall of sufficient strength and height to prevent the overflow of and damage to said City from the Gulf.

     II. That each of the members of said Board of Engineers so appointed has accepted said appointment and agreed to render his best skill and services in the matters aforesaid for the compensation stipulated and agreed to be paid him by said Board of Commissioners.

     In witness of all which the members of said Board have subscribed this memorandum and the President of the said Board of Commissioners has also subscribed the same for and on behalf of said City, this fifth day of December, A. D. 1901.

Henry M. Robert

written probably in the early 1900's. It seems to have been called forth by a controversy as to the relations between a president and the executive secretary of a church organization.

After rehearsing the details of the argument, Robert offers this broad statement of principle:

> "The great difficulty has been a misunderstanding as to what the generally accepted duties and standing of the Executive Secretary are. The difficulty has been that the Presidents have not realized that where there is an Executive Secretary, he or she is the executive officer of the organization, and that not the President but the Executive Committee is responsible for the policy of the organization. This difficulty has been greatly increased since last February when both the President and the Acting President thought they could instruct the Executive Secretary as though she were a five dollar a week clerk."

In this and in many other instances, the opinion of the expert was based on common sense and fairness quite as much as on the rules.

The spirit of the man is reflected in this bit of wise advice which he gave to one of his correspondents:

> "You cannot force people to agree with you. But when persons are approached in a conciliatory spirit, with an evident desire for the general good and willingness to yield personal preferences, where it can be done with no injury to others, I have found people responsive."

CHAPTER VI

Further Studies of Orderly Procedure

General Robert retired from active duty in 1901, with a long record of useful service. His retirement was not to idleness. The next ten years were filled with activities in engineering matters which he took on from a sense of duty, and in response to urgent demands.

During this period, his interest in parliamentary matters continued, as always, and he found time in the midst of his professional work to study further, and to carry on the extensive correspondence which resulted from his authoritative knowledge of the subject.

Concentrated study of his work became possible in the years from 1912 to 1915, when he applied himself to the task of completely revising the *Rules*. His added experience had given him a better understanding of the difficulties experienced by novices in applying the system he had provided, and had shown the need for enlargement of the treatment.

The result of these added years of work came in 1915, with the publication of *Robert's Rules of Order, Revised,* which is our standard, and no doubt will continue to be so. The new edition brought rearrangement and restatement of the earlier work, and it added nearly seventy per cent more material. Thus it became a greatly enlarged volume, and because of the new work it contained, a new copyright was granted.

Scott, Foresman and Company succeeded the Griggs Company as publishers of the *Rules* in 1896, and they have held that position ever since. They report that the book has achieved virtually world-wide circulation. While its authority is recognized throughout the United States, its influence is felt far beyond these limits. A Canadian edition has been issued, which has been freely circulated in Great Britain and the Provinces.

According to the publishers, orders have been received for the *Rules* from France, India, China, Argentina, Syria, Japan, Mexico, South Africa, and from every area in which the English language is spoken. Of course it does not necessarily follow that the *Rules* are fully authoritative in all these lands, but it indicates that the word has been spread, perhaps in large measure by American travelers, so that the book serves as a guide far beyond the boundaries of North America.

Thus the *Rules,* so carefully devised by Robert to facilitate the work of assemblies in the United States, have made their influence felt in many parts of the world, helping to promote democratic discussion and cooperation in public matters, and aiding people to "get at the will of the assembly."

The Revised Edition of 1915 brought no fundamental changes from the system presented in the beginning. The text was clarified as the result of the author's studies and critical comments from readers. The order of material was changed in some particulars so as to make it more convenient for quick reference, but the chairman who had learned his work in the editions of the 1890's had nothing to change when he took advantage of the improvements in the 1915 edition. The basic principles were unchanged. The structure so carefully put together in the days in Milwaukee has stood firm through all the years.

Up to the issuance of the Revised Edition, the sales of the book had reached nearly half a million copies. From that time until the centennial of the author's birth, May 2, 1937, that sales record had been equaled, so at that date the circulation had reached one million. Sales since 1937 have held to a high mark, and at this writing, in 1955, sales have reached a total of nearly 1,700,000 copies, according to information furnished by the publishers.

Interest in matters of parliamentary law seems to have been characteristic of General Robert's family. His work on the subject brought it vividly to their attention and caused them to follow his example. They became parliamentarians and made their contributions to the general good.

Especially helpful was the interest of his wife, Mrs. Isabel Robert, who labored faithfully in the process of revision of the *Rules* and in the writing of his two later books. General Robert's eyesight was failing through a number of years. He was afflicted with cataracts, and his extensive reading was difficult. Mrs. Robert became literally his eyes. She was his constant helper through the years, to the completion of these three great efforts. He was always able to write clearly, but often could not read what he had written.

His brother, Joseph Thomas Robert, Jr., took an intelligent interest and was able to assist the General at many points. This brother taught and wrote on parliamentary affairs, and among his products was a *Primer of Parliamentary Law*, the history of which deserves a place in this record.

He has told in some detail of his interest in providing a simplified interpretation of the material presented in the *Rules*. Like many another teacher, he felt the need for practical demonstrations of the principles. He realized that one cannot become a parliamentarian merely by listening to lectures and reading instructions. There must be the opportunity for practice. A more elementary work was desirable for use with inexperienced students. He prepared an outline of what he had in mind, and then took his ideas to his distinguished brother for discussion. In the preface to his *Primer* he has written:

> "When . . . I laid my rough plan for these 'First Lessons' before Colonel Robert, he said: 'In my opinion there is greater need of such a book than of anything else that can be written on parliamentary law. I have been trying for ten years to find time for writing such a book for practice of beginners, but professional duties make it impossible, and I am glad to have you take the matter in hand.'

"An essential prerequisite to making such a book as simple and easy as it ought to be is a few years' experience in teaching parliamentary law — to learn experimentally how difficult a study it is to most minds, and how little can be mastered in an hour.

"Through much tribulation and weakness of spirit, I think I've learned."

Joseph Thomas had been teaching classes in parliamentary procedure, and through this practical experience he had come to understand what kind of people he was writing for, and what their needs would be. His explanation of his method is worthy of our attention:

"The following pages have been written, cut to pieces, rewritten, many times during the past four years. I have divided and subdivided lessons, trying to make them so easy that a child must understand. I have tested them with class after class, club after club, and have simplified and illustrated each Rule anew, to make it still more clear to busy brains. If anywhere this little book makes parliamentary practice too simple and too plain, please let me know; and I'll give bonds to strive in all my future work to repeat that blunder as often as I can."

Joseph Thomas Robert not only taught classes, but he established a correspondence school in Chicago by which he extended the field of instruction. The title page of his *Primer* shows the author to be Joseph Thomas Robert, principal, the Robert Correspondence School of Parliamentary Law, Chicago, Illinois.

He was a careful student of the problems, seeking to discover the real needs of men and women so that teaching methods could be developed to give them maximum help. What the engineer had devised in theory, the teacher put to practical application. The contribution of this teacher must not be overlooked as we seek to give credit for the family's monumental service.

The publication of the *Primer of Parliamentary Law* in 1900 drew fire from some critics. So prominent a publication as *The Nation* printed a review of the book in its issue of June 21, 1900, together with an editorial which is given here, to show something of the change in sentiment which has taken place in the last half century. The editor of *The Nation* wrote:

"It is the author's purpose to make a textbook in parliamentary law so simple that the average high school teacher can make it plain to the average high school pupil. We frankly express our disapproval of the whole idea. However, we are ready to acknowledge that this Primer, which consists almost entirely of dialogues and examples to show methods of instructing high school boys, is very well prepared.

"Cushing's 'Manual' is generally accepted as an authority throughout New England and the Atlantic states. No new textbook is required.

"We shall dispose of Mr. Robert's heresies. His idea is to give every member of any public assembly such a smattering as will make him think he knows as much as the presiding officer. No better plan could be devised to cause trouble and reduce such meetings to riotous mobs. No assembly of any size can transact business properly unless it has full confidence in a presiding officer who shall be honest, impartial and thoroughly versed in principles and details of parliamentary law.

"One of Mr. Robert's fads is the idea that every motion must be seconded. In both branches of the Massachusetts Legislature it is especially provided by rule that no second is necessary. In the Common Council of Boston, the same custom prevails. The requirement of a second is unnecessary, and only leads to wrangling and to delay.

"Crocker's 'Principles of Procedure in Deliberative Bodies' and Cushing's 'Law and Practice of Legislative Assemblies' are standard authorities.

"The only real change in parliamentary practice during the last fifty years was made by Speaker Reed when he took the revolutionary measure of counting to make up a quorum, all members who sat in the room but declined to vote."

That editorial expression from the editor of an important magazine may be read with especial interest by the citizen of today, who believes that a general understanding of parliamentary procedure helps one to qualify as a useful member of an assembly, and that all members should have at least an elementary knowledge of such procedure. Instead of tending "to reduce such meetings to riotous mobs" we find that this knowledge helps to create an orderly atmosphere, and promotes decorum and courtesy on the part of all members of an assembly, with the possible exception of those who lack understanding.

One may wonder just where the editor of *The Nation* secured his complete information and the ideas which he expressed so dogmatically in his editorial pronouncement. Apparently he had not yet come in contact with the activities of Henry Martyn Robert, or else he had closed his mind against the intrusion of such disturbing ideas.

He was not the only one who thought that Joseph Robert had gone too far in the simplification of procedures. Various critics expressed their disapproval, but the people in general welcomed the chance to inform themselves, and the little *Primer* met with success. It came into wide use as an elementary textbook and its popularity continued for many years.

In recent years it has been displaced by the great number of publications on the subject whose better typography and better format attracted the attention of those seeking easy help. But while there have been great improvements in the arrangement of material and design of the books, no one has yet devised a better plan for helping people learn how to proceed than the simple method of going through the motions and practicing the procedures which Mr. Robert set up in his *Primer*.

He recognized the fact that the only way to learn parliamentary procedure is to practice it, in many meetings and in many actual or simulated situations. His book pointed the way.

During the years of revision, the thought of creating other books was taking shape in the mind of General Robert.

One of these came to completion and publication in 1921. This was *Parliamentary Practice, An Introduction to Parliamentary Law,* which was designed to give practical training in procedures. It was somewhat on the plan of the earlier work by Joseph Thomas Robert, but it elaborated on it by presenting first a chapter of discussion of a selected problem, and then a section of "Drill" on the subject. Thus, the first chapter deals with Main Motions, and the First Drill illustrates those teachings in an outline for handling matters in a meeting. The entire book is a presentation of the most practical method of gaining skill in handling the business of a meeting.

In the introductory section of this book, General Robert writes: "Ignorance of the rules and customs of deliberative assemblies is a heavy handicap to anyone who expects to influence the policy of a society."

He continues by pointing out the fact that without knowledge of such procedures, any person is comparatively helpless in an assembly where some of the members are skilled in parliamentary rules. Since it is customary for most of the people in a land of free speech and free right of assembly to be members of various organizations, it may be considered an essential part of the education of every person, even to the high school ages, to have some knowledge of how business is transacted in meetings.

He calls especial attention to the importance of using our knowledge only to help, not to hinder business, and he warns against the person who constantly raises points of order and resorts to other expedients to impede progress as being a hindrance and a danger to the democratic processes.

He makes another point of distinction as to the exact nature of parliamentary law which may help to clear up our thinking on the matter. He writes:

"The customs and rules usually governing deliberative assemblies in cases not covered by their own specific rules are commonly known as Parliamentary Law. These customs and rules came originally from England, but have been greatly modified by the practice of Congress and of State Legislatures, and especially by the practice of innumerable clubs and societies scattered over the United States. . . ."

A notable contribution was made by Henry Martyn Robert, Jr., a professor of mathematics at the United States Naval Academy at Annapolis, who became a parliamentarian of national reputation, serving as official parliamentarian for many organizations in their conventions. For eight years, he taught parliamentary law at the summer sessions at Columbia University.

Other members of the family also engaged in teaching and speaking on the subject, with excellent success in serving a large public.

Mrs. Henry Martyn Robert, Jr., has carried on the work of instruction since the death of her husband in 1937. She is in demand as parliamentarian in many conventions, and as a teacher of classes in parliamentary law. She has continued the family tradition of service by correspondence to those who encounter problems beyond their ability to solve.

For a number of years, General Robert cherished the desire to write a new book which was to be his really great achievement. He waited for the opportunity to come.

This book was to be no mere statement of rules nor codification of laws, but an authoritative volume showing in detail how an assembly is organized, how it gets its business transacted, and the reasons why things are done in the prescribed manner. He had in mind a work which would be a summary of his studies of the philosophy and methods of organized procedure. It was to be a sort of encyclopedia of parliamentary information.

This book, entitled *Parliamentary Law*, a volume of nearly 600 pages, was published in 1923, only a few weeks before the death of the author. While it has never gained the wide circulation of the *Rules*, it has been a valuable contribution to the literature on the subject, and it is perhaps the best and most comprehensive reference work for the earnest student.

General Robert's lifelong devotion to his church and to the Christian cause led him to make a special provision in connection with the publication of this volume. He directed that the profits from its sale should be contributed to the support of medical missions in China, a contribution which has been very useful during the years.

General Robert's experience as an engineer gave him a peculiar fitness for his task of building a system of parliamentary procedure which would stand up under all the tests of use. His military background gave him the basis for the creation of standard practice, invested with authority. Thus it appears that because he was an army engineer, accustomed to build on solid foundations and to make his structures of lasting quality, he was able to become the great parliamentarian of his generation.

Because of the close relationship of these two major interests, further consideration should be given to his work as an engineer. This was his chosen profession and his principal interest through the years when he was planning and erecting the structure of the *Rules*. But we find it easy to overlook the profession as we consider the tremendous results of the avocation.

Addison wrote: "Who does not more admire Cicero as an author than as consul of Rome?"

We may say, in our turn: "Who does not more admire and better know Henry Martyn Robert as the author of the *Rules* than as the army engineer?"

But we can hardly appreciate the Parliamentarian until we know something about the Engineer. For that reason, and because the story in itself is of absorbing interest, we must include the account of his greatest professional achievement.

CHAPTER VII

Robert Rebuilds a City

Following his service in the Great Lakes region, in 1882 the Major was advanced to the rank of Lieutenant-Colonel. From this time until 1890 he was Superintending Engineer of Fortifications and River and Harbor Improvements on the Canadian Border and on Delaware Bay. In 1889 he was appointed by the President to act also as a member of a Board of Engineers to study the problem of locating a harbor somewhere on the western side of the Gulf of Mexico. This harbor would be developed by the Government to handle the increasing tonnage, chiefly of cotton, from Texas and the south-western interior.

There was strong competition among the cities along the Gulf Coast. Such localities as Sabine Pass, Brazos River, Port Arthur, and Aransas Pass made vigorous campaigns. It was a matter of civic enterprise, supported by strong political pressure. There was need for a careful and unbiased study, and the thoroughness and impartiality of Colonel Robert made him an excellent member of the Board by whom the selection would be made.

It was thus that his connection with the City of Galveston began, a connection which was of great interest to him and of tremendous importance to that city.

With a clear vision of the ultimate possibilities of this development, not only to the cities involved but to the entire nation, Colonel Robert argued for a plan based on broader lines than those merely of local advantage. He foresaw the advantages of a port which would accommodate ocean-going

59

vessels of great size, requiring plenty of room and depth for their operation. His vision included the growth of a great center of world-wide commerce.

His estimate of the ultimate goal was a channel five hundred feet wide, with a depth of at least thirty feet. There would have to be shallower waterways on the sides, bringing the channel to a total width of two thousand feet. In addition, the flow of water must be such that, with the aid of jetties, the channel would maintain itself, saving the expense of constant dredging.

These specifications were not easily met, but after careful study of the proposed sites, he came to the conclusion that Galveston Island came nearest to meeting the need and that it was the logical location for the proposed harbor. His arguments were so sound and his figures so convincing that his colleagues on the Board concurred with his findings and agreed in recommending Galveston for the great development.

There was at this time a channel of considerable width, but with shallow water over the bars. Rival ports pointed to the lack of depth as a strong argument against Galveston, but Robert's recommendations included a plan for overcoming this obstacle. He seems to have applied his practice of detailed analysis to this just as in the case of the *Rules of Order*.

His study of the currents convinced him that with the construction of properly designed jetties, the channel would be dredged out by the natural forces, thus providing the needed depth and giving assurance that no future obstructions would occur. This fact gave weight to this recommendation.

Despite vigorous opposition, Congress approved the plan as recommended by the Board and appropriated the funds with which to start the work. It was this action which put Galveston on the map, and started it on the way to becoming the great city which we know today. The small town which had held on to its location through the years in spite of difficulties was now to have its chance to develop.

Even after the matter had been settled and the money appropriated, the discussion continued, and there were many

60

who predicted failure for the port of Galveston. The engineers stood by their decision, in spite of the gloomy forebodings of the losers.

Work on the jetties was begun in 1890. It was a tremendous task, and discouragements were abundant. During the five years which followed, the depth of the water on the bars increased but slowly, until in 1895 it stood at about fourteen and one-half feet, or less than half of what was required as a minimum. The question was whether there would ever be sufficient depth without a colossal task of dredging.

But Colonel Robert had been giving most careful study to the reports of the soundings. He found that the bar was steadily being forced seaward, and that while the front of the bar had advanced only two miles, the rear had moved up four miles. That is, the bar was being pushed out to sea, and at the same time it was gradually growing narrower. At that rate of progress, the entire bar would eventually be wiped out, and the problem would be solved.

There is a story told about an argument which involved Colonel Robert and led him to make some very definite and positive predictions. It was in May 1895, while he was on his way to Galveston by ship, that the vessel's captain expressed his opinion that it would be impossible ever to gain or maintain so much as eighteen feet of water over the Galveston bar. The Colonel retorted with a prediction that on December 31st of that year there would be at least eighteen feet of water over the bar.

Further than that, he said that there would be a gain of at least two feet a year until a depth of twenty-four feet had been reached. He was ridiculed, and it is said that even some of his colleagues, including General Comstock, believed that Robert had blundered in his forecast; but the careful engineer was sure of his figures. He had studied the contour of the Gulf bed and had observed the bar's rate and direction of movement. He knew that the body of the bar was getting into deep water and that the action of the currents would inevitably result in a rapid increase of the depth.

His confidence in his figures was justified when, on

December 31st, soundings disclosed the fact that there was a depth of nineteen feet of water on the bar. For the next three years the increase continued according to his calculations. Thus the low-lying strip of land which made up Galveston Island, thirty miles long and of no great importance, was reclaimed and turned into the center of a vast commercial enterprise. It is little wonder that the people of Galveston regarded Robert as being virtually the creator of their city.

Not only was he responsible for its coming into being, but it was by his engineering skill that the permanence of the city was assured. In 1900 Galveston suffered a terrible disaster when a violent storm almost swept the island and the city into the sea. For years the "Galveston disaster" was a conversation theme which ranked with the Chicago Fire and the Johnstown Flood.

We have a firsthand description of the event from Edmund R. Cheesborough, an honored citizen of Galveston, who served as a leader in civic affairs in the days of the disaster and who was influential in the work of reconstruction. His work in this connection brought him into close contact with General Robert and his activities in the rebuilding of the city.

Looking back on those days some thirty years later, Mr. Cheesborough wrote:

"On September 8, 1900, Galveston was visited by a terrific hurricane, the results of which shocked the civilized world. Thousands of people lost their lives, and the city itself was a mighty wreck. Under the old form of city government, a Mayor and a Board of Aldermen, elected from the respective wards, the business of the commonwealth had been badly managed, and the storm left it practically bankrupt.

"After some delay, a lot of hard work and patriotic effort on the part of leading citizens, we adopted what is known as the commission form of government for our city. A Mayor and four Commissioners, elected from the city at large, took over the direction of affairs. One of the first acts of the commission was to engage three engineers of marked ability to design a system of protective works that would make the city safe from serious damage from storms.

"The City Commission secured the services of General Henry Martyn Robert, Chief of the Corps of United States Engineers at Washington, who had just been retired. Associated with him were Alfred Noble, then President of the Society of Civil Engineers of the United States, and H. C. Ripley, formerly City Engineer for Galveston, and at one time a U.S. Engineer. General Robert was chairman of the Board.

"The studies made by this commission resulted in a report embracing the construction of a magnificent seawall of a special design, seven and one-third miles in length, together with the elevation of the grade of the entire city through the use of twenty-five million yards of dredged material.

"A red granite monument on top of the seawall at the foot of Tremont Street bears an inscription showing that the wall cost $6,501,132, of which the Federal Government paid $2,600,000, the balance being borne by Galveston County. The cost of elevating the grade of the city was $5,908,000, paid by a bond issue. This twelve million dollar project has fully prevented the city from storm damage to this day.

"Later on, General Robert visited Galveston as consulting engineer in connection with other public works. He was an engineer of marked ability and sound judgment — a patriot — a big hearted, up-standing, highminded gentleman. His services were of the greatest value, and all Galveston honored him and called him 'Friend'."

In view of these facts, it is not unreasonable to suggest that the city of Galveston stands today as a monument to the genius of this great engineer and builder, a monument impressive enough to satisfy the ambition of any man.

The story of the Galveston Seawall is one of the epics of American history. While it has been of primary interest to engineers and builders, even the casual tourist can hardly fail to be thrilled by the sight of this structure which has successfully challenged the power of the sea and demonstrated the ability of science to cope with the threat of nature.

To realize the magnitude of the undertaking, one must understand the problems which were to be met. To appreciate it more fully, one must realize that General Robert approached the task with the same keenly analytical attitude which had characterized his work on the *Rules.*

General Robert and his fellow engineers on the committee were called upon to handle the entire problem of safeguarding the city against the danger of damage from future tropical storms. This involved the raising of the grade of the entire city to a level above the reach of high waters and the provision of drainage, projects which did not offer insuperable difficulties. The other matter was the hard one: to devise a breakwater or seawall of such strength and height that it would prevent overflow and damage in all circumstances.

There were three fundamental points in this seawall project. First, the barrier must be strong enough to stand against the heaviest tides. Second, it must be anchored so that no water could get underneath and dislodge it. Third, it must present a face to the waves which would discourage them from overflowing onto the land, and would tend to throw water back into the Gulf. These were engineering problems calculated to challenge the best resources of science.

The design which resulted from months of study and calculation was so simple that one need not be a trained engineer to understand it, but the creation of the plan marked a new accomplishment in the engineering field.

There was to be a massive concrete wall, sixteen feet wide at the base and five feet wide at the top. It extended to a point seventeen feet above low water mark, and the base was placed well under water. The sea face of the wall was to be curved, so that its lower part would provide a means of deflecting the waves by giving them an upward turn. The upper part was to be made vertical, thus impelling the water to fall backwards instead of spilling over on to the land.

Rows of heavy wooden piles were to be driven far down into the soil, to furnish a solid foundation for the base of the wall, and a great layer of riprap twenty-seven feet wide and three feet deep, made of tremendous blocks of stone, was to be placed on the seaward side of the base. It was believed that this very substantial obstruction would be sufficient to turn back the fury of any storm which might attack the island and the city.

The quality of the work has been tested on several occasions during the years, and it has stood up to every test. There was a storm in 1909 which was little less dangerous than the great one of 1900, and there have been other extremely severe attacks on it, but nothing has caused serious damage.

One interesting test of the quality of workmanship and materials used in the structure occurred in the storm of August 16, 1915. During this cyclone, a four-masted schooner was blown completely over the wall. It was dragging two heavy anchors, and these caught on the top of the wall, where the schooner was soon pounded to pieces. The damage to the wall consisted of two chips, each of about two cubic feet of concrete. Citizens to this day take pride in pointing out these marks as evidence of the strength of their protecting wall.

The world marveled at the spirit shown by the people of Galveston, which was called "the pluckiest city in the world." They marveled likewise at the genius shown by the engineers who designed the seawall, to whose effectiveness the city owes its safety.

Older residents of Galveston, who remember the events of the past, have a deep sense of appreciation for General Robert and his associates in giving them protection, but those of the present generation have but a dim idea of the disaster and the courageous reconstruction which followed it. Most of the people, if they mention his name, call him "Roberts" just as most of the rest of us do.

For the person who knows the facts, the city of Galveston, with its protective works, stands as an enduring monument to the engineering skill of General Robert, even as the *Rules of Order* is a memorial to his devotion to the cause of freedom and fairness in discussion.

While these two accomplishments are thus comparable, the fact remains that the building and preservation of Galveston, with all its importance to commercial development, is by no means equal in widespread influence and usefulness to the little brown book which for so many years has been the authoritative guide for organizational action and which, in fact, qualified General Robert for the title of "The Great Peacemaker."

CHAPTER VIII

Years of Retirement

During the later years of his active service, Robert served on many boards and commissions, usually in connection with his special interest in river and harbor work. He taught, lectured, and advised. His work took him into all parts of the nation, thus adding to his wide and interesting acquaintance, and bringing him into vital contact with many who had come to know him through the *Rules*.

Having reached the age of retirement, he was relieved from active duty on May 2, 1901, after being commissioned Brigadier-General.

This retirement marked the close of a long, honorable life of service in the United States Army, but at the same time it brought the coveted opportunity to carry forward the studies in parliamentary matters, and to give to the world the benefits of his studies and observations in this field. His interest in this subject never slackened, and his later writings preserve for us the results of this continued study.

Active and alert until the last, General Robert was a man of tremendous energy and of almost unlimited capacity for work. No doubt he subscribed to the thought of Benjamin Franklin, who wrote: "Energy and persistence conquer all things." He kept his strength to an amazing degree for a man of his age.

In a letter to a friend, written in 1920, when he had passed his eighty-third birthday, he said:

"My friends tell me that they have never seen me looking better. I presume it is due to the physical work of this summer. We bought a house last summer, and have been at work remodeling it for six months, sometimes with nine carpenters, plasterers, masons, plumbers, etc., at work at the same time. As the work has been done by day labor, it has required constant oversight."

It is easy to imagine this venerable engineer as he directed the reconstruction of his home, with a knowledge of detail which must have surprised the workmen.

It has been said of him by intimate friends that he had no hobbies aside from his love for useful occupation. He was always seeking to learn something or do something which would be worth while. This did not prevent him from entertaining other interests, however.

He found great enjoyment in his home, especially in teaching his grandson to sail, play pingpong, and how to engage in other activities. He was intensely interested in photography, and he had in his home all the equipment for developing and printing his pictures, at which he was expert.

The last weeks of his life were spent in a sanitarium in Hornell, New York. The end came on May 11, 1923. The body was returned to Owego, for funeral services in the Baptist Church before being taken to Arlington National Cemetery for burial.

Dressed in the uniform of his rank as Brigadier-General, he was interred with full military honors in this necropolis for the great ones of the nation.

The passing of so notable a personage might well have attracted nationwide attention, but a careful search of the periodical literature of the time reveals that not much was printed about it. The magazines and reviews, together with the newspapers, missed a rare opportunity to pay tribute to a great man and his great work.

Possibly the fact that parliamentary law is generally considered a dry and uninteresting subject may have led to the impression that the man who devised the American system of procedure must have been as colorless and uninteresting as the subject. Perhaps the newsmen of that day did not connect the engineer with the parliamentarian in their thinking. Whatever the reason, General Robert's death was given very little attention by editors and writers.

One newspaper, the *Minneapolis News,* was an exception. This paper published an editorial tribute which shows a true appreciation for the General's service. In the issue of May 14, 1923, this newspaper characterized the life and work of the author of the *Rules* in this paragraph:

"Millions of people have been for years under obligation to this quiet and efficient military man. He was the author of 'Robert's Rules of Order,' which has been for more than one generation the accepted authority on parliamentary procedure, and which has smoothed the way for the conduct of legislative business throughout the land. Every work on parliamentary debate published in the last quarter century has been based on the fundamentals established by Robert. It would be interesting to know how much time has been saved by the little book that can be carried in one's pocket. It is hardly too much to say that this little volume has preserved the possibility of sanity in debate and it is certain that it has preserved the possibility of social amenities amidst argument. To do one thing supremely well is honor enough for one man. General Robert did one thing so well that it will never have to be done over again."

But what about the man himself? We would like to know what kind of man it was that did so great service in two fields.

Information about his military activities is not difficult to obtain, since his achievements speak for themselves. But dependable information about the man himself is less easily available, since most of those who knew him intimately have passed on.

Between what they have said or written about him and what we can gather from his writings, we are able to form a fairly accurate picture, although it is unfortunately lacking in detail.

We know that he was a man of dynamic personality, energetic and strong both in mind and body. His early bout with the Panama fever affected his health for a number of years, but later in life he made a complete recovery from its effects, so that his strength was equal to the heavy tasks laid upon him.

In spite of distinguished honors, he remained a modest, rather retiring man. He was alert and enthusiastic in his interest in events, and he tried to keep abreast of the times. His deeply religious nature showed itself in his loyalty to his church and in his readiness to help in the advancement of its endeavors in service.

An informative note is included in a sketch which appeared in *The Engineering News Record,* in the issue for April 22, 1920. The editor, Mr. E. J. Mehren, had spent a few days in Owego, visiting with General Robert and gathering material for the article. He wrote his impression of the aged officer in these words:

> "Energetic, strong in mind and body; heaped with honors, but nevertheless extremely modest; enthusiastic, interested in the events of the day; a sane optimist, and above all a sterling character.

> "Today, despite the fact that his 83rd birthday is nearing, the General is hale and hearty — his mental powers undiminished, his physique still equal to fairly hard work. In conversation, he habitually sits on the edge of his chair, a trait characteristic of the enthusiasm he puts into all that he does."

General Robert was much in demand, not only as a parliamentarian, but as a leader and teacher in Christian work. Among his papers are found briefs and outlines for sermons, Bible studies and miscellaneous talks before Christian organizations. Just for example, let us note the outline for a speech delivered before the Nashville Y.M.C.A. on Sunday, 3:45 pm. April 17, '93. The subject is "The

Word of God — Its Supreme Purpose." The outline, as given in his handwritten notes, is this:
"to teach men how to become like God.

(a) It is not to teach History, Geography, Chronology, Science or Art.

III: The Printing Press, Steam Engine, Telegraph, etc. if taught by Jesus to disciples —

(b) It is not to teach simply Salvation. Many Christians stop at conversion; our churches are filled with weak, sickly Christians.

(1) The fear of God is the beginning of wisdom

(2) Unless ye be born again

(c) It seeks to make men God-like, fit for companionship with God. It does this by precept and example."

The outline closes with a series of examples: Abraham, Joseph, David, Daniel, Jesus, Paul.

Another outline shows the plan for a sermon delivered on July 5, 1902, at Haworth, New Jersey. His text was the first verse of Psalm 103: "Bless the Lord, O my soul, and forget not all His benefits."

He began with "Yesterday was the Fourth of July, the birthday of our nation" and then proceeded to speak on the reasons for gratitude on this patriotic occasion. The sermon "heads" were:

"(1) The foundation of our nation, in a practically uninhabited country, with opportunities for development. Compare with the experiences of the Israelites entering the Promised Land.

(2) Peace, and the growth of the nation.

(3) Preservation of the unity of the nation.

(4) The opportunities afforded by immigration, bringing great numbers of people under the influence of our Christian civilization.

(5) The conclusion: "What shall I render unto the Lord?" We must work to evangelize the great mass of our population, and show them by our lives the character of true religion."

This sermon bears the note: "thirty minutes" which may indicate to us that General Robert was keenly aware of the importance of timing, even for a sermon.

One other document which deals with the General's effectiveness as a churchman is a set of resolutions adopted on the occasion of his removal from a community where he had taken an active part in the activities of his church. The appreciation runs in part thus:

"At a meeting of the Jenkintown Baptist Church, held this Saturday evening, March 12, 1904, the following resolutions were adopted:

Having learned with deep regret of the intended departure from our midst of General Robert and wife, we, the members of the Jenkintown Church, the officers of the Sunday-School and the members of his class, and friends at this meeting,

RESOLVE, That in the departure of General Robert and his wife, after their most pleasant and congenial stay among us, this church loses most efficient workers, earnest helpers in all the spiritual work of the church,

That from the time they have come among us, they have taken up the work willingly and heartily, and assisted us in lines that, heretofore, we have not been able to pursue . . .

That we have been exceedingly benefited by the General's lectures on the Bible and the very clear way that he has expounded the Word.

That he has given us many ideas that we shall never forget."

There is another revealing note in a letter which Robert

wrote to Professor J. G. Pate, President of Boscabel College, Nashville, Tennessee, under date of April 25, 1893. It appears that he had been invited to deliver some lectures on the Bible to the students of the college and that a question was raised as to payment for his services. He writes:

"You speak of compensation. I have had all the compensation I expected or desire in the consciousness that I have done what I could to stimulate the students to study the Bible. A man who knows anything is in debt to those who are less fortunate, and he can only pay the debt by imparting the knowledge. If he gives his life to this work, he must be supported by it, but business men who earn their support in other ways should freely give their services to help elevate mankind."

People who knew General Robert as a friend and an associate described him as a kind-hearted, friendly person, although a stern disciplinarian. He was firm in matters which involved considerations of right and wrong, and when he had reached a decision, after adequate thought, it was hard to change him.

He was a man of compelling enthusiasm. He was a marvel of concentration when some matter claimed his attention, and he was such a thorough and painstaking student as one would expect a man of his profession to be. His thoroughness in study was not limited to his profession, but reached into all his many interests.

General Robert seems to have combined the firm, fact-finding, scientific attitude with a disposition that was not only fair and generous, but even gentle and genial. He won friends readily, and kept them permanently. It must have been a privilege to know him as a friend and neighbor.

His sense of fairness and appreciation for others was reflected in the military order already referred to, issued while he was on duty in the Northwest. In this, he recognized the value of opinions and ideas from other people. He may have violated military traditions when he invited the men under his command to help with their suggestions, but he exhibited a degree of wisdom and tolerance far ahead of his time.

He was married twice, and he owed much to the help of the two splendid women who shared his life. Mrs. Helen Thresher Robert, his first wife, took an active interest in the work of her husband, and was a ready helper with suggestions and comments. It was her suggestion, as has previously been noted, which turned his thoughts to the importance of giving practical explanations of the application of his theories in common use. At any rate, we are indebted to Mrs. Robert for having thus spoken in our behalf.

General Robert became a widower in 1895. In 1901 he was married to Isabel Hoagland, who was his constant companion and helper during the years of his retirement. She gave invaluable help in handling his correspondence and in the task of compiling the revised edition which marked the climax of his work on the *Rules*. He would have been the first to acknowledge his debt to these two women for their confidence and their active assistance.

On February 19, 1951, the seventy-fifth anniversary of the publication of the *Rules*, Mrs. Isabel Hoagland Robert and the General's daughter, Mrs. Dewitt Clinton Redgrave, presented to the Library of Congress a first edition of the *Rules*, together with a copy of the 75th anniversary edition. At the same time, they handed over to Luther H. Evans, Librarian of Congress, a collection of manuscripts, scrapbooks, and correspondence from the records of General Robert. These materials are thus available for study by persons interested in the development of our accepted system of procedure. Much of the material presented in this account of General Robert's work has been secured or verified by reference to these records.

So far as the American people in general are concerned, General Robert might be classed as one of the "forgotten men." We have used his *Rules* and have known his name, usually miscalling it "Roberts," but we have not identified the man nor thought of him as a person. We have been very stingy in the building of monuments or placing of tablets in his honor. No one until now has even taken the trouble to record the simple facts of his life so that they might be known by those who follow his teachings.

But if we have failed in the erection of monuments, he has not been left without an appropriate memorial. His own work is a finer and more useful reminder than anything which we could construct of bronze or marble. The City of Galveston stands as a record of his skill and genius as an engineer, and his book lives to perpetuate his name wherever men and women meet in their societies. His influence is felt whenever someone arises to say, "Mr. Chairman!"

*   *   *   *   *   *   *

"No one is ever strong and forceful when he gets near the limits of his knowledge. A teacher should know far more of a subject than he ever expects to teach. A leader in any deliberative assembly should be prepared for every emergency, so that there is no danger of his being tripped up by some expert parliamentarian. While this knowledge greatly increases one's efficiency, it is not wise to make a display of it, or to use it in a way to interfere with carrying out the wishes of the majority of the society. Where there is radical difference of opinion in an organization, one side must yield. The great lesson for democracies to learn is for the majority to give the minority a full, free opportunity to present their side of the case, and then for the minority, having failed to win a majority to their views, gracefully to submit and to recognize the action as that of the entire organization, and cheerfully to assist in carrying it out, until they can secure its repeal."

Henry Martyn Robert, *Parliamentary Law.* (page 4)

CHAPTER IX

Appendix

The following sections are presented as an interpretation and a commentary. The purpose is to make very clear certain points which are frequently misunderstood or overlooked, even by those who are deeply interested in matters of procedure.

1. *The Rules are Simple.* This is an effort to encourage the novice who becomes discouraged as he contemplates the apparent complexity of parliamentary procedure.

2. *The President* needs encouragement and information about the important functions of his office. If this discussion of his duties helps him to a better understanding and a more effective performance, it will have accomplished its purpose.

3. *The Secretary* may fail if he does not understand just what are his responsibilities. There is nothing particularly new in this study, but even an experienced secretary may gain some helpful ideas from it.

4. *Standardization* is one of the conditions of modern life. It is no less essential in the conduct of organized business than in the manufacture of machines and appliances. This chapter may help to a better understanding of the reasons for keeping parliamentary practice in a fixed and permanent form.

THE RULES ARE SIMPLE

Anyone who has gone through the first ten pages of the *Rules of Order*, (skipping, of course, the twenty-four pages of preface and introductory remarks, as is our custom) will challenge that statement about simplicity.

By the time he gets through "Obtaining the Floor" and has reached "Motions and Resolutions," his brain is in a whirl, and he is ready to toss the book aside and let nature take its course when he next gets into a meeting. This is the natural result of trying to take too big a dose of strong medicine all at one time. Parliamentary skill or understanding is best gained by taking one item at a time, putting it into practice, and making sure of it before going on to the next order of business.

There are certain elementary and comparatively obvious facts about procedure which should be known to every person who participates in organized activity. These facts or principles really are simple. If they are understood, even the novice can get along. If he does not comprehend them, he will run into embarrassing complications, and may feel that he is being treated unfairly. The following matters are most elementary, and yet some of them are overlooked or disregarded by many people who should know better. Read them calmly and without fear or prejudice. Fix them in your mind, and then you may approach the next meeting of your club with confidence.

The first fact is that any member of the assembly is entitled to speak when he has something to say which is pertinent to the occasion, and when someone else is not speaking. The first step is to secure permission from the presiding officer. This permission is necessary, not because the president or chairman is a dictator, but in order to maintain order and decorum in the meeting.

To obtain permission to speak, rise and address the officer by his title. Say, "Mr. Chairman" or "Mr. President" or "Madam Chairman" as the case may be. Note that the right way is to rise and address the presiding officer. Some people even today choose to remain seated, with upraised hand, or with snapping fingers to attract attention, but this is not done by those who really know their procedure. The raised hand is reminiscent of the schoolroom. The person desiring to speak should not be too modest or too busy to get up on his feet.

If it is in order for you to be heard, the chairman will respond to your "Mr. Chairman" by calling your name; or in a small meeting he may merely indicate his recognition by a nod of the head or a wave of the hand. Then you "have the floor" and are at liberty to speak.

In speaking, you should either be offering a motion, or presenting a resolution or a report, or speaking upon some motion or matter which has previously been introduced.

When you have spoken your thought, as briefly and as clearly as possible, sit down. You have had your turn, and you are not entitled to speak again until all others who wish to talk on the matter have had their opportunity. Then you may ask for recognition in order to present further remarks and say the bright things which you forgot to mention the first time you were on your feet.

If you are presenting a motion, you will secure the floor, and then state the motion clearly and in the form you wish it to be. If some explanation is required, you may speak briefly before presenting the formal motion. Otherwise, wait until it has been seconded, and then ask permission to discuss it.

General Robert holds that every motion, except very brief and routine ones, should be written, and that the copy should be handed to the secretary when the motion is made. That is a good rule to secure accuracy, but it is much too frequently overlooked. Then it becomes the duty of the secretary to write the motion so that he has a record of it when called upon to state just what it says, after lengthy discussion has obscured the wording.

Writing the motion is a great aid to brevity and clarity, and it promotes intelligent thinking on the part of the mover.

When the discussion of a motion appears to have been completed, the chairman puts it to a vote. He does not need to wait for someone to shout, "Question! Question!" All that is necessary is for him to inquire, "Is there any further discussion?" Lacking any immediate response to his question, he proceeds to call for the vote, saying something like, "If there is no further discussion, all those in favor will say 'Aye'. Those opposed will say 'No.' "

The chairman judges the result by the sound of the voices, and announces that the motion is carried or defeated on the basis of what he has heard.

If anyone is not satisfied that the chairman heard correctly, he may call for a "division of the assembly," which means a vote by rising or by the showing of hands. Details on this procedure are to be found in the *Rules of Order*, pages 189 and 190, reference to which is advised in case one is uncertain about it.

When you offer a motion, remember that the correct form is to say "I move" that so and so be done. Make the wording of the motion very clear and concise, to avoid misunderstanding.

Remember that the approved form is to say, "I move" rather than "I move you" or "I make a motion." Some people just cannot get away from the habit of saying, "I make a motion." There is nothing illegal about it, but that is not the best wording.

This is a good place to emphasize the choice of words by repeating a little story on the subject.

It appears that at a political meeting in the hills, a participant in the discussion was shot by several of the others in attendance. This incident on the open floor created considerable comment in the village.

A stranger who happened to be in town asked an acquaintance, who had been present in the meeting, just why the shooting took place.

The native explained: "The fellow made a motion that was out of order."

"What!" the stranger exclaimed, "you mean to tell me that they shot a man in cold blood just for making a wrong motion?"

"Well," drawled the other, "the motion he made was toward his hip pocket."

As an example of a proper motion, well worded and clear, consider this one: "I move that a part of each meeting of our society during the next two months be devoted to the study of parliamentary procedure."

Now let us put the same idea into a form calculated to infuriate and bewilder any presiding officer to whom it is presented; and let us remember that a great many motions are offered in a manner quite as confused and mixed up as this:

"Mr. Chairman, I move that our club take up the study of parliamentary procedure if we can find someone to teach us who won't charge too much and that we make this study a part of every meeting for the next few weeks until all of us get a better understanding of how to carry on in our meetings, because there is so much carelessness in the way we have been doing things that half of our actions must be illegal."

You have heard motions like that, a mingling of argument and explanation which obscures the real intention and makes the proposal so indefinite that no member can vote intelligently on it.

If you were presiding, what would you do with this kind of motion? There are several possible courses which may be followed, depending on what seems desirable at the moment.

You can ask the mover to re-phrase it so as to make it understandable.

You can reword it yourself, saying, "As I understand it, the intent of your motion is this:"

You can let the motion as it stands be seconded and discussed, and when the time comes for the vote, you can call upon the mover to re-state it more clearly.

A great waste of time can be avoided by getting a motion properly stated at the first, and much confusion and misunderstanding can be removed.

Mention is made of the "second" to the motion. Bear in

mind that before a motion is properly "before the house" for discussion, it must receive a "second" from some person other than its introducer.

Seconding a motion is very simple. The person wishing to give his support may remain seated, simply calling out, "Mr. Chairman, I second the motion!"

After a motion has been offered and seconded, the chairman must state it; that is, he says, "It has been moved and seconded that . . ." Then he asks if there is any discussion of the matter proposed in the motion. This is the signal for those who favor or oppose the motion to take the floor in orderly fashion and present their arguments. It is all just as simple as that, if the chairman keeps his head.

If the motion is found to be unsatisfactory in any respect, the member finding it so may offer an amendment. To do this, he secures recognition and presents his proposal for a change, offering the reason for this action if it seems desirable. The proper motion is: "I move to amend the motion by . . ." whatever changes he wishes to suggest.

An amendment may be made by striking out, or adding, or inserting words or phrases, or by changing the wording of the motion. The mover should always specify the exact changes to be made by the amendment.

The amendment takes precedence over the original motion for discussion and voting. That is, the amendment must be disposed of before the main motion can be voted on. If the amendment is adopted, it becomes a part of the main motion, which may again be discussed and then voted upon.

When an amendment to a main motion has been disposed of, it is in order to offer another amendment for consideration and vote, but there must never be more than one primary amendment and one secondary amendment before the meeting at one time. That is, there can be an amendment to the motion, and then an amendment to the amendment, but no motions beyond this are in order.

It is easy to see why this is so. Multiplication of amendments could run the entire matter into such condition that the only solution would be to invoke the rookie's command:

"As you was before you was as you now is."

In voting, the second amendment is taken up first. If adopted, it becomes part of the first amendment, and if the amended amendment is then adopted, it is all incorporated into the main motion.

We have devoted considerable space to this one phase of business because there is so much misunderstanding and need for clarification about the matter of motions and amendments.

Another matter which frequently troubles the inexperienced chairman is the "point of order."

There may be some member of the assembly who thinks that the rules are not being properly followed. He has the right to arise when the breach of order occurs and say, "Mr. Chairman, I rise to a point of order." The presiding officer will say, "State your point of order." The member will state his point, and then the chairman will rule on the question. After considering the matter, he may say either, "The point of order is well taken, and we shall do whatever is needed to correct it," or he may say, "The point of order is not well taken."

This decides the procedure to be followed. If matters are out of order, they will be corrected. If the point is not well taken, matters will proceed as before. But if the objecting member is not satisfied with the ruling, he will rise and say, "I appeal from the decision of the Chair." Any decision of the chairman is subject to appeal, but the appeal must be made promptly after the ruling is announced.

The chairman then may say, "An appeal has been taken from the decision of the Chair. As many as will sustain the decision will say 'Aye'. Those who will not sustain it will say 'No'." He will then be guided by the vote. Or he may state, more formally, the question at issue, giving his reasons for the decision if he thinks that is desirable. Then he will present the question in this fashion: "The question is, shall the decision of the chair stand as the judgment of this assembly?" or, "Shall the decision of the chair be sustained?" The vote decides the question. Questions of order and appeal are fully covered in the *Rules,* pages 78 to 83. Look it up for yourself.

Always, if the vote goes against his ruling, the wise chairman will accept it cheerfully and will not show resentment. His business is to follow the will of the assembly and not to enforce his decisions.

These suggestions cover the simple conduct of business. A proposal is presented in a motion, which must be seconded. When it has been stated by the chairman, it is open for discussion. When discussion has been completed, the vote is taken, and the result is announced by the chairman. If amendments are presented, they are handled as outlined. The chairman must always be careful to see that every proposition, motion, or amendment is voted on.

But business is not always so simply disposed of. There are many variations, many pitfalls for the unprepared president. He must know what to do in various circumstances. This is where his copy of the *Rules of Order* will be brought into use.

The table of "Order of Precedence of Motions" which appears in the front part of the *Rules* will be found most helpful if it is understood. In recent editions, this table comes inside the front cover. In older ones, it follows the Table of Contents. It is not necessary to memorize these tables, but it is most desirable for the chairman to be so familiar with them that he can turn quickly to the needed reference and get the information at a glance.

Another necessity for the parliamentarian is to be familiar with the complete and detailed Index which is found at the back of the book. Bold face type sets out the principal heads so that they are quickly found, and the subheads list all entries under each classification.

If you will tackle it in the right way, and proceed with reasonable care, you will find that the rules really are simple.

Take up each division separately, one at a time, and study it through until you get the idea. Do not attempt to master all the details at once, and most particularly do not attempt to memorize everything.

It is worth while to have a clear understanding of the differences between incidental motions, privileged motions, and subsidiary motions, and to know in general about the precedence of motions, but for most of the details you can quickly refer to the *Rules* index, if you have become familiar with it. Don't overburden your mind. If you get into a position of confusion, you can always ask for time out to look up the point you do not understand.

Let us take a quick review of the matters presented in this section. These you must have in mind, whether presiding or speaking from the floor:

1. To obtain permission to speak, address the chairman.
2. To speak, you must either be making a motion, or presenting a resolution, or speaking upon a motion already made.
3. Do not attempt to speak a second time on the same subject until all the others have had their say.
4. When you offer a motion, make it clear and brief.
5. The seconder of a motion does not have to gain recognition.
6. Any main motion can be amended.
7. Not more than two amendments can be pending at one time.
8. A motion to adjourn takes precedence over all others if unqualified.
9. A member who disagrees with the chairman's ruling may appeal.
10. The chairman may call for a vote on sustaining the decision or the appeal.

THE PRESIDENT

The president of any assembly is the one, literally, who "sits out in front." That is the exact meaning of the word in its Latin form, *praesidere*. (Latin *prae*, before, plus *seder*, to sit.)

Other titles are applied to him, according to the preference of the organization. He may be the chairman, occupying *the* chair in the meeting. Other members may sit in chairs also, but the chairman has the chair of office or of honor, from which he conducts the meeting.

In some assemblies he is known as the moderator. In this capacity he may be expected to serve as an arbitrator or umpire or controller, who guides and restrains.

When the presiding officer is a man, he should be called "Mr. President" or "Mr. Chairman" or "Mr. Moderator" as the case may be. If the president is a woman, she is addressed as "Madam President" or "Madam Chairman" or otherwise, as indicated by the official title.

Whatever his title may be, the president's duties are quite plain and simple. He serves primarily to keep things moving in orderly fashion, making decisions as to procedure and guiding the work so as to get the business done in a prompt and democratic manner. He is not a "boss" nor a dictator. He is primarily the servant of the organization. Tact and courtesy are his characteristics. To these he should add good judgment and an open mind.

Sometimes there appears to be an impression that the one chosen to be president is thereby miraculously endowed with almost infinite wisdom and power. When he becomes president, he may think that he has all knowledge and understanding, and that his word is law. His will must not be thwarted.

That may be what *he* thinks. He will learn better, or he will have a miserable time.

Any person who takes office with the notion in his head that he is going to run things is foredoomed to disappointment and failure. People do not like that kind of procedure. If he is presiding over an assembly of plain speaking, clear thinking people who know their way about, he will find himself checked, corrected, and generally put in his place.

The duties of the president may be considered from three aspects. First, he presides over meetings of the society. Second, he presides over certain committees, such as the executive committee, or the board of directors, or governing board. Third, he coordinates the work of committees or other groups charged with special tasks for the organization. He does not step in to do the work of the appointed committee chairman, but he makes certain that the chairman does his duty.

In addition to his responsibilities as chairman, the president becomes the representative of his organization on the outside, in the community, and in cooperation with other groups. This is a very important task, for it is by his appearance and performance that others judge the organization he represents.

As a chairman, the duties of the president are quite lucidly set forth by Robert in the *Rules*.

Here we find that the president's first business is to call the meeting to order at the appointed time, not half an hour late, and not even one minute late. He comes before the assembly with the order of business before him, and he announces the business to be considered in the order in which it should be acted upon. If any special matters are to be considered, outside of the ordinary routine business, he will have at hand the agenda, which has been prepared in advance in conference with his Executive Committee. He recognizes speakers, states motions which are offered, conducts the discussion, and puts matters to vote. After the voting, he announces the result.

When discussion is under way, he mildly restrains the members, keeping them within the established rules of order and enforcing the observance of order and decorum. When questions of order arise, he makes the decision, always subject to an appeal.

His rulings are not arbitrarily given, but are always based on the principles of right and justice, and on the accepted rules of procedure. The assembly may reverse his rulings by a formal vote, in which case he gracefully accepts their decision. In all things, according to Robert, he obeys the commands of the meeting or the organization as expressed in its corporate actions.

As a matter of practice, the president is supposed to

stand when he puts a motion to the vote and when discussion is a matter of short speeches by various members who desire recognition. When a lengthy talk is being made, he takes his seat and relaxes. In smaller groups or in the case of informal meetings, he may sit or stand as he prefers, but he must always be in the position to direct the meeting. There should always be someone in charge of affairs.

The president is entitled to vote when the voting is by ballot, and in other situations when his vote will change the result, either by creating a tie or by breaking it. If there is a motion which refers definitely to the president or chairman, this should be put to the vote by the vice-president, the secretary, or by the maker of the motion, thus sparing the chairman the embarrassment of calling for a vote of thanks or censure for himself.

In no case does the president have a right to cast more than one vote.

A wise president never takes advantage of his position to enter into a discussion, or to interrupt speakers except in matters of decorum and order. If he wishes to talk about the question under debate, he calls another member, preferably the vice-president, to take the chair for the time being, while he, the president, secures the floor and speaks on the level with the other members. He does not assume the chairmanship again until the matter under discussion has been disposed of.

The importance of maintaining at least the appearance of neutrality is emphasized by Robert in these words:

> "If the chairman has even the appearance of
> being a partisan, he loses much of his ability to
> control those who are on the opposite side of
> the question . . ."

There are many other wise words by General Robert which should be heeded by every person who serves as chairman. The earnest student is referred to section 58 of the *Rules*, beginning on page 236, which deals at length with the conduct of the chairman or president. Read with especial care the paragraphs in fine print, beginning on page 240.

No better advice for a chairman has been given than that which is carried by the dictum that familiarity with parliamentary usage is not enough. There is need in addition for some degree of leadership ability, and of capacity for controlling others. "He should set an example of courtesy, and should never forget that to control others, it is necessary to control one's self," is a sentiment which should be kept in mind by every presiding officer.

The "Hints to Inexperienced Chairmen" on page 242 are all too frequently overlooked by those who most need them. They can be read with great profit by even the most inexperienced chairman, and certainly should be studied by the one who lacks experience.

Sometimes a presiding officer, swayed by a sense of the importance of his position, is tempted to "show off" his superior knowledge of procedure. He may get by with this unless some members of the group have a thorough understanding of the matter, in which case they can easily embarrass him.

The intelligent chairman will keep in mind the words of an eminent English writer on parliamentary law, who is quoted by General Robert as having written:

"The great purpose of all rules and forms is to subserve the will of the assembly rather than to restrain it; to facilitate, and not to obstruct, the expression of their deliberative sense."

The president, then, needs to realize the nature of his position which is that of a guide, an umpire, and a leader; never a dictator nor an arbitrary ruler. He develops plans, in consultation with his fellow officers, and he proposes what he believes to be wise action, but he is always more concerned about securing thoughtful and unanimous action by those over whom he presides than he is about getting his own way.

Tact, open-mindedness and courteous consideration for the opinions of others are characteristics of the good chairman. To these he must add a reasonable understanding of parliamentary procedure.

Robert makes one sweeping statement of opinion in these words:

> "The presiding officer of a large assembly should never be chosen for any reason except his ability to preside."

This opinion will find many dissenters in regular practice, for there are, quite obviously, other essential qualifications; but the ability to preside impartially, courteously, and intelligently is essential to successful chairmanship.

The opportunity to serve as president or chairman of some worthy organization is something to be desired by any ambitious man who is willing to be of service. It is an experience calculated to reveal and develop latent qualities of leadership; and to broaden the scope of life for the man who serves faithfully.

The man who seeks the position of president for purposes of self-gratification and personal glory is headed for trouble. The ideal president is the one who realizes that, while he "sits out in front" or leads the forward march of his organization, he is still the "servant of all."

THE SECRETARY

The title of the recording officer, like that of the president, is of classical origin. The Latin word *secretum* means a secret, and it is the source from which our word secretary is derived. Thus, the secretary may be counted "a keeper of the secrets" of the organization.

The ordinary society does not have many deep and carefully guarded secrets, but it does have documents and records, and the secretary is the officer who keeps these records and other papers which pertain to the business and activities. He is variously called clerk, scribe, recorder, or some similar title, according to the preference of the society. The term does not greatly affect his responsibility.

Very definitely he is the historian, for his records show what happens in the meetings, and from his books it should be possible to gather information about the organization from its beginning to the present moment.

Laxity on the part of a secretary in keeping complete records and in preserving these records through the years sometimes leads to the loss of such important information as the list of charter members, the names of early officers, the exact date of organization, and even to the disappearance of the constitution and bylaws, with amendments. Not only does a good secretary know the "secrets" but he must keep these items of information safely and in order, so that his successors may know and understand the backgrounds of their work.

Primarily, the secretary keeps the records of the meetings, usually referred to as the minutes, or the journal. In addition he keeps the correct roll of the members, the constitution and bylaws and standing rules, the lists of committees, and the correspondence files.

He attends to correspondence unless there is a special corresponding secretary. He sends out notices of meetings and performs many other tasks which are assigned to him, either by the organization's rules or by the president or the executive committee. An efficient secretary is a busy person, and he has remarkable opportunities for experience and training in useful activities.

Since keeping the minutes is one of the most important tasks, special attention is here given to this responsibility. What should be included in the minutes and what omitted? How are the minutes to be preserved? How are they made official?

The main purpose of the minutes is to show just what has been done, and when and by whom.

Brevity is a desirable quality, so long as it does not obscure the meaning. Long, wordy descriptions of discussions and enactments are not good. In fact no record of discussions and arguments is required unless some exceptional circumstances make them important. The minutes show what is actually done, not all that is said by the member.

There is no place in the minutes for personal opinions

or for "editorial" comments on the part of the secretary.

The first item in the minutes is the date and kind of meeting; that is, whether it is a regular or special or adjourned meeting. The fact that the president was in the chair, or the name of his substitute if the president is not officiating, should be shown. The minutes always show just who presided.

The approval of the minutes of the previous meeting is shown, or if the reading was dispensed with, that is noted.

Reports of committees are mentioned, any essential details or recommendations being included.

Main motions and points of order and appeals, and all other motions which were not lost or withdrawn, are shown in the record. The last statement is to be taken with some judgment and discrimination. There are some motions so unimportant that they hardly deserve a place in the record, but any motion which substantially affects the business of the organization must be included. Sometimes the fact that a certain motion was defeated is as essential to the record as the fact that another was adopted.

The secretary may properly place on record the names of persons offering motions of importance. He may or may not add the names of seconders, depending on his judgment as to the importance of doing so. No harm is done by including these names.

Brevity and accuracy are two essentials in keeping the minutes. The accuracy may be questioned or sustained by the other members when the minutes are read for approval, and they are not to be considered as finally official until the members have had the opportunity to express themselves.

It is not necessary to have a motion to approve the minutes. The chairman can save time by saying, after the minutes have been read, "Are there any corrections to the minutes? If there are none, they will stand approved as read." If corrections are offered, they may be included by common consent, or a vote may be taken, if there is difference of opinion.

Sometimes, when important business has been transacted, it may be desirable to have the minutes completed and read at the close of the meeting, for immediate approval. If the assembly has entered into controversy, the wise secretary will ask for the privilege of presenting the record right on the spot, so that he may be assured that his reporting is accurate.

The secretary is an important official. His responsibilities are serious, but they should not be onerous. His duties are shown in considerable detail in the bylaws of the organization, and he should be thoroughly familiar with these rules. He does not properly follow his own preferences, if those preferences are in conflict with the rules of the society.

Like the president, he is a servant of the organization, and in his service he is the faithful recorder of their actions.

He is not so prominent a figure as the president, but frequently he is responsible for the efficient working of the president, keeping him informed about matters which require attention, and warning him if he strays beyond the limits of the rules. He is the president's right hand man, and the organization's faithful scribe and historian.

For a detailed and most helpful explanation of the work of the secretary, refer to the *Rules*, pages 244 to 251.

STANDARDIZATION

Most of us are inclined to resent regimentation. We claim the right to choose our own ways of doing things. We are free agents.

In spite of this, every one of us is daily restrained by observance of standards, adopted in the interest of ease and efficiency of operation. Without this means for facilitating action, we would be hindered and even crippled in most of our activities. Uniformity promotes freedom of action.

For example, a generation or two ago, every manufacturer of hardware and machinery used his own ideas about the size and style of fittings and parts. Screw threads of many varieties were employed. If you purchased fittings of some one brand and tried to use them with fixtures of another make, they did not fit.

The manufacturers saw the need for uniformity, and they agreed on certain standards to be used by all. As a result, you can today buy fittings for your garden hose with assurance that they will fit, whether you buy at a plumbing shop, a dime store, or at the corner grocery.

Seventy-five years ago, the railroads used a variety of track widths. The rolling stock of the New York Central would not run on the tracks of the Rock Island Road. If freight was to be shipped to some point not on the line of the railroad which first took it over, the entire consignment had to be unloaded from the one and reloaded on the other, because the freight car could not be switched from track to track. Commerce could not be handled today without the standard practices. The value of uniformity is too obvious to require argument.

Consider one more example of the importance of standardization. In the United States, people turn to the right when driving or walking. Traffic holds to the right side of the highway. In England the custom is exactly the opposite. The driver stays on the left side. So long as everyone follows the custom, it makes very little difference which side it is, but the American, driving for the first time on British highways, has a difficult time trying to conform to the rule which contradicts all his habits and training.

The same reasons which make it desirable to have uniform fittings for garden hose may be applied with equal force to the matter of procedure in public assemblies. There are many sizes and types of screw threads which could be used, one of them as good as another, but by selecting only one and agreeing on its universal use, we get satisfactory results.

Parliamentary rules might be changed with great variety, but the changes would throw us once more into confusion unless all of us agreed on them. Uniformity in usage is almost as vital as having the right principles to follow.

One of the great contributions made by General Robert was the production of rules of procedure which were so logical and practical that the public could be brought to accept them, thus making the usage universal. In some instances he could have adopted other practices quite as good as the ones he did select, but some final choice had to be made, and he used the ones which seemed to him to be the best for all considerations. Then the public adopted them.

Whether we shall move the previous question or limit the number of amendments or admit substitute motions or vote with black and white marbles placed in a golden urn is not so important as that we shall all do the same things in the same way.

Robert's *Rules* constitute a complete, logical, and well integrated system of procedure, which has been so widely accepted that any radical changes would constitute an impediment rather than an aid.

It is true that the *Rules* have no legal authority, nor any other authority except such as is accorded them by the people who appreciate their value and choose to be governed by them. Any individual has a right to make his own rules, just as any organization has the right to determine the rules under which it will operate. Your society could make the secretary the presiding officer, and could require its president to keep the records, if that was the desire of the majority. But would anything be gained by that except confusion?

Uniformity of practice is a matter of vital importance in a day and a land where so many people belong to so many organizations, and carry on so many activities which require orderly procedure. Without agreement upon the rules to be followed, we would quickly revert to that chaotic condition which inspired Robert to formulate his system.

General Robert never made the claim that his system is the only one or even the best one that could possibly be devised. He held that some system which can be universally agreed upon and used was a necessity if people were to work together intelligently, and he believed that his system, being simple, logical and practical, was worthy of general acceptance. It seems to have impressed other people, too, as being acceptable and usable, and so it came into its

94

present wide use, making it possible for people from all parts of the land to conduct their affairs harmoniously and efficiently.

In these times, when great national conventions are held, with thousands of delegates in attendance from all parts of the country, imagine the situation if the delegation from Texas and the delegation from Minnesota insisted upon following their own local rules of procedure, while those from New England or Georgia or Montana claimed favor for theirs. No business could be transacted until some agreement had been reached.

Many organizations have their own special variations in procedure and in terminology, which are quite all right so long as they are understood and accepted as individual organizational practice, but it would be unwise for any organization to adopt extensive or basic variations unless there are compelling reasons for doing so. Different organizations use different titles for their officers. In one, the presiding officer may be the "Grand Universal Potentate," while in another he is merely "Mr. President." The difference in titles does not seriously change the official duties. The secretary may be known as "the scribe" or "the recorder" or "the keeper of the seals," but his responsibilities are about the same, whatever we call him.

In the case of procedure the situation is different, and most organizations stay faithfully with the *Rules,* to their great benefit.

Some enthusiastic teachers of parliamentary law have advised their students to discard some of the restrictions laid down by Robert. As a rule, their criticisms are based upon personal prejudice. Whether their ideas would prove helpful or harmful if put into general use may be questioned, but the fact that confusion would result from such changes is not to be denied.

One popular writer and teacher has written: "Why limit us to two amendments to a motion? Why not have a dozen, or twenty?"

The question answers itself in the mind of any person

who has had experience with the maze of multiple amendments. The ordinary chairman has trouble enough with one or two. Give him half a dozen to wrestle with and he will be "sunk without a trace."

Furthermore, it is evident that any motion which is so carelessly worded as to require a great number of amendments should be ruled out at the start, with instructions to the mover to put his ideas into intelligent form before he brings them forth for discussion.

Uniformity in parliamentary procedure is not an undesirable form of regimentation. It is a necessity in such a nation as the United States or Great Britain, where people so readily assemble from all quarters for conventions, and where every society is likely to include a mixture of members from diverse points of origin. Such uniformity, instead of hampering, promotes freedom of movement and discussion.

Let those who are tempted to disregard Robert's *Rules* in favor of some personal preference take time to consider whether their independent action may be calculated to increase efficiency, or to throw us back into the state of confusion from which Robert rescued us.

Until someone is able to offer a new system so much better than the present one that it will win general and immediate acceptance, as did Robert's plan, let us stand by the principles which he gave us.

The important point for us to remember is that in any meeting the fundamental purpose is to determine "the will of the assembly" and then make that will effective. The procedure set up by General Robert works effectively to that end. By our clear understanding of his method and our faithful practice of principles, that purpose may be fully accomplished, and the rights of free citizens will be preserved.